a SMALL BOOK ABOUT GOD

HIS WAYS, HIS DREAMS, HIS PROMISES...FOR YOU

ROY HICKS JR.

MULTNOMAH PUBLISHERS
SISTERS, OREGON

A SMALL BOOK ABOUT GOD

published by Multnomah Publishers, Inc.

© 1997 by One Way Ministries

International Standard Book Number: 1-57673-072-7

Cover design by Jeff Gelfuso

Cover photo by Raymond Gehman/National Geographic Image Collection

Printed in the United States of America

Unless otherwise marked, Scripture quotations are from:

New American Standard Bible (NASB) © 1960, 1977 by the Lockman Foundation

Also quoted:

Scripture quotations marked "NKJV" are taken from the *New King James Version.* Copyright ©
1979, 1980, 1982 by Thomas Nelson, Inc. Used by permission.

All rights reserved.

The Holy Bible, New International Version (NIV) © 1973, 1984 by International Bible Society,
used by permission of Zondervan Publishing House

The King James Version (KJV)

"It Is Good to Praise the Lord" and "The Promises of God," copyright © 1987
One Way Ministries, Eugene, Oregon. "Praise the Name of Jesus," © 1976 Latter Rain Music,
The Sparrow Corporation—all words and music by Roy Hicks Jr. Used by permission.

For information:

MULTNOMAH PUBLISHERS, INC.

POST OFFICE BOX 1720

SISTERS, OREGON 97759

Library of Congress Cataloging-in-Publication Data:

Hicks, Roy.
  A small book about God/by Roy Hicks, Jr.
    p.cm.
    ISBN 1-57673-072-7 (alk. paper) 1. Sermons, American. I. Title.
BV4253.H53 1997
252--dc21   97-24107
                                                                       CIP

97 98 99 00 01 02 03 04 — 10 9 8 7 6 5 4 3 2 1

CONTENTS

A WORD FROM KAY HICKS

The title of this book was chosen by my late husband, Roy Hicks Jr., prior to his death in an airplane crash several years ago. He never finished *A Small Book about God*, but this was the title the Lord had impressed upon him before he died.

I am very grateful to Eileen Mason, Evelyn Wheeler, and Jim Thomas for their labors of love in reconstructing this sampling and collection of Roy's sermons. They have taken his powerful delivery style and put it into a written format that captures his anointed spirit and the life-changing impact of his teaching upon our church. A special thanks also to Pastor Steve Overman, Russ Pierson, and Beth Barone.

Roy and I served together in pastoring Faith Center in Eugene, Oregon, for nearly twenty years, during which time it became a Mother Church, birthing more than fifty pioneer churches that are still serving scores of people today.

My thanks to David Kopp, Melody Carlson at Multnomah Publishing, and Faith Center for their editorial support and encouragement in creating this gift to the Body of Christ. My prayer is that this book will be a blessing to the "larger Church" of Jesus Christ in the same way that Roy helped all of us become "larger people" within the Kingdom.

FOREWORD:
A MAN OF INFLUENCE

I loved Roy Hicks Jr. During our adult lives, hardly a day went by that he didn't check to see how I was doing, and then offer a few words of encouragement and love. If you've never met my friend Roy, I'd like to introduce him to you.

The setting was Eugene, Oregon. A desperate and depressed woman had gone to the Ferry Street Bridge to take her life. She related in the local newspaper what saved her; saying that Roy "showed up out of the blue" and talked her out of jumping. She said, "If it wasn't for him, I'd be dead right now."

Roy was always making a difference in the lives of those around him: family, flock, a friend, or someone he'd never met before. Someone from a distance could easily attribute that to Roy's amazing array of personal gifts and abilities. Anyone who walked close to him recognized the remarkable quality of the presence, the love, the wisdom, and the power of Jesus Christ. God had simply chosen to endow Roy's life with a special measure of grace that equipped him for an incredibly broad and influential ministry. He was a pastor, a teacher, a pastor of pastors, and a leader of leaders.

I think you'll discover *A Small Book about God* is something like potato chips. You can't eat just one; and once you start reading, you won't be able to quit. Roy studied the Word with the exegetical precision of a surgeon and practically applied it to people's lives like a world-class tailor chalks, cuts, and stitches a suit for a meticulous personal fit. This anthology of Roy's sermons is a real treasure. Whenever Roy spoke or wrote, it was so personal to me—almost as if he had eavesdropped on my prayers or read my mail.

I'm glad you'll get to know Roy a little as you read. He always touched and exposed the depths of my soul. I hope that within these pages you'll sense an invitation to know Jesus Christ as never before. I also pray that you'll respond. Nothing would delight Roy Hicks Jr. more than that.

RON MEHL
ROY'S FRIEND

PART ONE

A Promise
for You

THE PROMISES OF GOD

The promises of God
will surely come to pass.
I'll stand upon His word
and trust and see how faithful
He will be who died for me.
For He exalted His word
above all His name.
The promises of God
will surely come to pass.

ROY HICKS JR.

1
"I MAKE ALL THINGS NEW!"

God doesn't make all things new by changing the outside.
He wants to remake the substance of our lives.

One bleak January afternoon, as I left my office to go home, I found myself up against a blustery winter rainstorm. Icy fingers of rain and wind seemed to want to remove my overcoat. But as I stepped off the curb, a strange thing happened. I suddenly thought: "It's spring! Spring is in the air!"

That was such a ridiculous thought I laughed out loud.

As I ran toward my car, I started fumbling for my keys. I mentally kicked myself for not getting them out of my pocket before I left the building. While digging through my pockets, I tried hard to keep some papers dry that I had tucked inside my jacket. But the gusts of rain ruined that plan. At the car, I lost a few more seconds trying to figure out which way to turn the key. By the time I crawled into the car, everything was soaked, and I was frozen.

Then, out of nowhere, the thought ran through my mind again: "Spring is in the air…" And I laughed again. But this time another thought dawned on me: "Maybe I'm not fantasizing about dry weather and sunshine. Maybe the Lord is trying to tell me something."

At home I sat thinking in my office. I began to feel that the Lord truly wanted to show me something new, something fresh in the middle of winter. After a while, I reached for my pencil and started a list.

New covenant. New creature. New song. New name. The phrases kept coming. *"Your mercies are new every morning." New commandment. New man. Newness of life, and newness of spirit.*

I opened to Revelation 21, where John describes his vision of the new heaven and new earth. In verse five, God speaks out of eternity into time. This is what He says: "Behold, I make all things new."

As I sat there in my study, still very wet and cold, that proclamation kept ringing in my heart. God was talking out of eternity about a future event—but He was also talking about the present too. About this time and this place.

A NEW KIND OF NEW

God, eternal God, is the One who in every circumstance longs to make new. Our human definition of *new,* however, is so very different from God's. King David's approach to transporting the Ark of the Covenant (2 Samuel 6) is a good example of how most of us think about *new.*

David wanted to bring the sacred Ark to a permanent home in Jerusalem. He decided the Ark deserved a special ox-drawn cart, not the hand-carried method detailed in the laws of Moses. But David's good intentions quickly turned into a big mistake when the oxen stumbled and the Ark threatened to topple off. As a bystander reached out to steady the Ark, he was struck dead. David wanted to improve on God's plan, but his human perspective of newness was different from God's.

In the everyday circumstances of life, the best choice so often seems to be the new thing—new career, new job, new wife, new car, new home, new city, new start. But our concept of newness goes about as deep as that new car smell—persuasive and delightful, but how long does it last? Invariably, when we want new, we play around with the outside while the inside stays the same.

Yet the outside isn't the problem.

God doesn't make all things new by changing the outside. He wants to remake the substance of our lives. When God summons a soul, it's not a one-time event; He calls us to something new every day. We get all excited about self-improvement, but God doesn't really seem to be in the improvement business. He prefers to get to the core of the problem. He is the God of change. So when God says, "Behold, I make all things new," think about... *You.*

Think about the person you are. Think about your character or personhood. So you see some room for improvement, some need for propping up here and there? I have tremendous news for you. God is not a fixer. He is a Creator! The One who speaks out of eternity into your specific moment has a very personal message for you: "Behold I make *all* things new."

> *God is not a fixer.*
> *He is a Creator!*

A NEW THING NOW

Many of us who have been through loss or failure treasure Isaiah's words about newness: "Do not remember the former things, nor consider the things of old. Behold, I will do a new thing, now it shall spring forth; shall you not know it? I will even make a road in the wilderness, and rivers in the desert" (Isaiah 43:18–19, NKJV). That day in my study these words came to me with new power and insight.

If God is speaking to you right now about newness, maybe He is gently saying, "Forget the past. Don't dwell on what's behind you."

Or maybe in the midst of your trying circumstances, His word to you is, "I am about to accomplish something completely new."

Or maybe He is trying to tell you something even

more personal: "Behold, I will do a new thing in you *now!*" The Lord wants so much for you to see it, to recognize it when it comes.

You might be looking at your situations or relationships and saying to yourself, "Impossible! There is no way anything new can come for me." Yet, perhaps the Lord is saying to you, "Where there seems to be no way, where there seems to be no resource, I will make a road in the wilderness, or in the desert I will cause rivers to spring up."

Why am I so certain about the message of newness? Because impossible circumstances and blustery January afternoons don't change who God is. The God of eternity promises you and me that He is the One— the only One—who is in the business of making everything new.

Four simple instructions out of these two verses can help you to cooperate with the new thing God wants to do in your life.

1. LET GO OF THE OLD

Let's face it, we get pretty good at digging ourselves into very deep, comfortable holes. We'd rather hide in the easy, or hold tightly to the familiar, than reach for the genuinely new. We don't really know how to start over because the necessary and the optional, the fresh and the stale, the good and the not-so-good-anymore are all wound around each other, and around us, down in that comfy hole.

My advice is simple: Let go of it all—the bad *and* the good! I see two sides to letting go—a passive and an active side.

The passive side has to do with surrender: "I'll drop it. I'll let it be taken out of my hand. I refuse to hang on to it." God wants to do a new thing, but He can't as long as you tenaciously hang on to the past. Identify what is stale and stagnant in your life. Yes, it was a good thing when it first began, but even good things become spoiled, worn out, and weak. Resign from it. Leave it behind. Let go of it. So many old things in our lives will fall away of their own accord if we'll only unclench our grip, open our hands—and keep them open.

But some old things must be forcibly ejected. In 2 Corinthians 4:2, Paul talks about actively letting go when he writes: "I have renounced the hidden things of shame." The mind naturally jumps to heinous sins—robbery, murder, or some sexual sin. But Paul is talking here mostly about a dishonest way of living—a lifestyle based on manipulation and selfishness, those unseen motives of the heart. These attitudes and behaviors are never going to leave just because you open the door.

Action is required—yours! Let go of the old. Better yet, kick it out!

Paul's word *renounce* implies more than just saying no. In Greek, "to renounce" has legal implications. It means to say no *again* to something that you've already said no to, forbidding access to something you have previously forbidden. Renouncing might sound like this: "Years ago I said I wouldn't have that in my life, and I kicked it out. Now, as I'm living my life, minding my own business, it shows up again. Maybe it's an area of vulnerability or a weakness in my character, or possibly it's just the cycle of life that has brought it around again. But that thing that I said no to before is standing right here! It has stolen in again—or wants to. Right now, I must deal with it again. I see it for what it is, and I say no. I meant no before, and I mean it again—*No!*"

To renounce, as Paul uses the word, is to be willing to say no the second time. This is actively letting go.

You have made a strong commitment to Jesus, but I encourage you to look at what's thriving—or threatening to thrive—around the edges of your life. Some unwanted "weeds" you've already said no to are there again. Renounce them. Say no the second time. If you want to be in that place where God can do His lovely work of newness in your life, then get rid of the old. Something better, something new, cannot happen until you do.

> *If you want to be in that place where*
> *God can do His lovely work of newness in your life,*
> *then get rid of the old.*

2. GET READY

The second simple instruction is not profound, but it's important: *Get ready*. Peter's spin on this would be, "Gird up the loins of your mind." I would expand his advice in these ways: Get ready to run. Get ready to move. Get ready to change location. Get ready to adjust…

Be ready now!

Some can relate to what it is like to watch a young son or daughter learn to compete in sports. Kids can be more interested in having a good time than in winning. I remember when my son Jeff was learning to guard his man in basketball. He would look around to see how his buddy was doing or look over to see if his parents were watching. At those times, he wasn't taking the game very seriously. Sometimes as he was moving down the court, I'd yell at him, "Get your man!" or, "Get in position now!"

Some of us play the game of life the way our kids play sports. We're not taking the game very seriously. And when the ball is thrown—if we even see the ball—we're sometimes just not ready.

I want to candidly and lovingly say to you, "Get

your head in the game. Be ready! Where's your man? Get in position—the ball is coming your way. Wake up, sister! Wake up, brother! Come on now!"

God says these kinds of words to us because He loves us, not because He wants to say things that will hurt us or throw our game off. God doesn't want to bench you. He wants you to get your head in the game.

Do you want to receive the new thing God has for you? Do you want to make sure it doesn't pass you by? Then get ready!

3. DO THE POSSIBLE

Remember the woman who thought, *If I can just touch the hem of His garment, I shall be made well* (see Luke 8:41–56)? Luke's account, interestingly enough, implies that she was saying over and over, "If I can just touch the hem of His garment…If I can just touch the hem of His garment…"

She did the possible—and received healing. That healing, of course, was something she could never have done for herself. But she accepted the responsibility for the possible and left it up to Jesus to accomplish the impossible.

Remember the four men who wanted to bring their crippled friend to Jesus? They tore open a hole in the roof to get him to the Lord—an extraordinary but very possible action. Who did the healing? Jesus. He forgave the crippled man, then healed him—and the man got up and walked away. His friends took responsibility for the possible. Jesus took care of the impossible. That's a law of life.

Funny how easily we reverse that law, especially in our marriage relationships. We attempt the impossible when we try to change another person or when we fight against a reality that is going to exist whether we want it to or not. In the process, we can nearly kill our relationship—or our spouse! What's possible then? We can always choose to say something nice, send a card, make a call. We can pray. We can encourage. These possible things—and there are countless more—make way for the impossible to happen.

Imagine that you meet the blind man in Jerusalem soon after Jesus has smeared mud over his eyes. He walks by you, feeling his way through the streets and alleyways. You can hear him muttering, "I need to go to the pool of Siloam. I need to go to the pool…"

Just then, you notice a helpful bystander rush up to the blind man, "Hey, you with the mud on your face," he says, "I have a jar of water right here. Let me help you wash off."

That's when you hear the blind man say *with conviction in every ounce of his body,* "No, no, no thank you! Jesus told me to go to the pool of Siloam and wash it off. That's exactly what I'm going to do!"

The blind man with mud on his face walks awkwardly, even foolishly on, toward the pool of Siloam. He is accomplishing the possible, that's all. But he is on his way to receiving something new and impossible from God—the miracle of sight.

Read the Gospels. It's there again and again and again. Do the possible. When you sense Him instructing you, stay away from everything else. Do the possible thing He asks you to do. Let go of everything else.

And as the impossible begins to take place, accept and recognize it as God's work, not yours. Look for ways to cooperate with what He is doing.

4. MOVE WITH THE NEW

Even after God has spoken a guiding word or given us a promise, we may easily miss the thing when it finally begins to happen. We know He's going to do it. We set ourselves to pray and wait. But when God begins to "birth" that promise into reality, we often miss all the signs.

Meet Elijah. In 1 Kings, chapter 18, God tells the prophet Elijah that He is about to reveal His power to the rebellious King Ahab (1 Kings 18:1–46). First, God sends fire from heaven to destroy the prophets and the priests of Baal—right before Ahab's eyes. Then in answer to Elijah's prayer, God sends a rainstorm to end a terrible three-year drought. But watch how the story unfolds—while Elijah prays for rain, his servant goes up on the hill seven times looking for approaching clouds. Nothing. Not even a wisp—until the seventh time.

The servant comes back from his seventh trip to tell Elijah, "Master, there is a cloud there, but I tell you it's only the size of a man's hand."

Elijah's response is very instructive. "Get up," he tells his weary servant. "Go tell King Ahab he'd better get back to the palace. There's a deluge coming."

All of that from "a cloud the size of a man's hand." Did you catch it? That moment of recognition where you know. Like Elijah, you seize it in faith. "That's it," you say, "and I'm going to move with it."

The moment of recognition—when you realize that God is doing something new—can be the point of releasing what He is trying to do, or it can be the opposite. The releasing, or the hindering, always starts in the same place—your mouth! Remember that the psalmist says, "I lay my hand over my mouth so I will not transgress." He understood that life and death are in the power of what we say, especially at those first stages of newness.

Is there a new thing happening in your marriage? Protect and bless it by carefully chosen words. Do you see a small beginning (perhaps just "a cloud the size of a man's hand") in your personal life today? Get ready, take a possible step. Is something new developing in your little nine-year-old, or that sixteen-year-old? Move with it.

Birthings are moments of both promise and vulnerability. God is trying to prosper and bless you. By your words—and by your decision to move with Him—you can be a part of bringing His miracles into being.

Just step off the curb of your life, roll your collar up against the freezing rain—and let go with a laugh. Spring is in the air, and at this very moment the God of new things is summoning you to your destiny.

LORD, DO A NEW THING IN ME

Lord Jesus, You are the God of the impossible who says, "Behold I make all things new."

I trust you, Lord, to make my deaf ears hear. To make my blind eyes see. I see the old, but in my life I want the new.

By Your great power, enable me to open wide to receive Your spring in the middle of my winter, O God of new beginnings. Amen.

2
THE MAKING OF A DREAMER

The God of eternity has something in mind for your life that has been in His heart from before the foundation of the world.

If you were candid about the personal dreams you have for your life, would you say life has turned out to be all you had hoped? Or is it something less?

All of us have our dreams, and at one time or another, most of us have experienced deep disappointment in the pursuit of those dreams. You may have given up your dream. Perhaps you've even become a skeptic, resenting anyone who tries to rekindle hope that God might have a dream for your life.

But the Bible is clear: God does have His dream for your life—things for you to do and things for you to be that move you toward your destiny in Him. Are you ready to receive God's new work in this deep part of your soul?

When believers lose their sense of destiny, they become spiritually impaired. In fact, we need a dream to survive. Proverbs 29:18 tells us, "Where there is no vision, the people perish (KJV)."

We use the word *dream* in many ways. Great visionaries pursue dreams that can change whole cultures.

Those we call dreamers are often fools chasing unrealistic fantasies. Of course, all of us dream at night. Most of us have personal dreams of what would make us happy or fulfilled.

But I am not talking about any of these meanings. In fact, part of our difficulty in grasping God's dream for us comes from not realizing that, for the most part, His dreams for us have very little to do with what we want, or with what will make us happy.

You can never reach for the kind of dream God has in mind for you. It is always received. That's one of the chief ways you can tell if it is truly God's dream for your life. Let me explain.

The God of eternity has something in mind for your life that has been in His heart from before the foundations of the world. Psalm 139 reveals that God knew you intimately before you were even formed in your mother's womb. In those scriptures, the psalmist speaks of a deep sense of destiny, of assignment. His assignment is eternally significant. When God calls you to a new thing, He has something important and specific in mind. God's hopes and plans for you are not trivial or second best. God's dreams are about being and doing. About achievement and accomplishment. About destiny and calling.

These are God's dreams for you. Taken together,

they are God's unique assignment for you that gives meaning and purpose to your life.

But you may say to me, "I've already tried to find my dream, my assignment, and I've only been disappointed." You may even have decided that it's much easier just to live life without a dream. But your Father in heaven wants more than that for His children. God's eternal plan is in motion. He is up to something. And He is inviting you to be a part of it, to experience all that He originally intended for your life. God accomplishes this work in your life through the presence and power of His Holy Spirit as you listen to His leadings and follow His directions. It is through the Spirit that you discover your *assignment* and *personal portfolio—places to go, people to see, things to accomplish.*

What makes it possible for people like you and me to believe there's something for us personally, individually in God's economy? What are the essential requirements for becoming a person of vision, a person who possesses—and lives out—his spiritual birthright?

The truths we need to grasp are well illustrated in the life of Joseph, a man famous for his dreams. As we observe his life, starting in Genesis 37, we can lay a foundation of understanding that will enable God to restore your God-given privilege to dream.

DREAMING WITH GOD

Our story begins when Joseph is just a boy. Out of eternity, God starts to shape and prepare Joseph to carry a dream that will position him to become a savior for the Jewish nation. God speaks to Joseph in vivid images while he sleeps, and plants seeds of vision and identity in the heart of a young man. What God deposits into the heart of Joseph during the night hours becomes a part of his hope and expectation.

Later when Joseph is betrayed by his brothers, sold into slavery, and unjustly imprisoned, his dreams seem to have ruined his life. But God is up to something—carrying out His plan to rescue the Jewish people.

God's dream for us may complicate or even radically rearrange parts of our lives. That can be difficult for us to accept. But our life stories and the stories in the Bible have this in common: On the surface, the dream is about us, but if our dream is God-given, it will always ultimately be about God. God's plan is in motion, and we get to be a part of it.

The Bible tells us about God's people—where they went, what they did, how they responded. But all of it points to a revelation of *who God is,* and *what He's up to.* In the same way, when you take hold of a real dream, a dream from God, you'll still be the star, the principal player. But your dream from heaven will have more to do with who God is and what He is up to than it will ever have to do with you.

This idea is not only a difficult reality, it is a life-changing truth. And it is critical to catching God's dream for you. We are given the marvelous privilege of participating in God's work on earth. But Christianity is not first of all about us. Christianity is about Jesus Christ. The same is true of the dream God has for our lives. We will see how all of this plays out in the life of Joseph.

> *On the surface, our life story is about us,*
> *but if our dream is God-given, it will*
> *always ultimately be about God.*

FAVORED TO DREAM

Jacob particularly loved his young son Joseph, born to him by his dear wife, Rachel. And out of this great love, Jacob blessed Joseph with a distinctive gift—a tunic of many colors. The coat might have been unusual simply because of its fine array of colors, or perhaps because it was a ceremonial coat that would ordinarily have been reserved for the eldest son. Regardless of its precise significance, it was a sign of favor. So much so that it stirred up tremendous jealousy in the hearts of Joseph's ten older brothers. You can imagine how they reacted when "Daddy's Favorite" unwisely told them his latest dream, a dream that seemed to imply that these older brothers would someday bow down to him. They hated him even more.

Joseph knew that he lived in a place of special grace in the eyes of his father. It was a grace and favor that was not built on performance but issued completely from Jacob's heart.

One thing is certain: Regardless of what you may or may not have experienced as a child growing up in the home of earthly parents, your Father in heaven provides an environment of total acceptance for you as His child. It is an amazing environment to grow up in! In Ephesians, Paul tells us that we have been accepted in the Beloved, and that we have become His cherished sons and daughters. In Jesus Christ, God makes possible this favored place, this place of total acceptance. Just like Jacob with Joseph, God's favor rests upon you as His "highly favored one." This is true of every single person who is born again into the family of God.

It is this acceptance by the heart of a loving God that sets you free to achieve. Because you are accepted, you can now excel, your performance can now be Spirit-led with the possibility of eternal consequences.

Whenever performance is elevated above the truth of acceptance—whether it's in the home, in the church, or in your own mind—you are not free to dream. Any sense of destiny or assignment from God is stifled.

Because you are accepted and esteemed, God has an assignment chosen specifically for you. The assignment isn't measured by how well you've done. It isn't measured by what you've earned. It has to do with the simple fact that God has put His love upon you. You're a favored one.

FLOURISHING IN FATHER'S LOVE

Now let's take it a step further: Not only was Joseph the *favored* son, he was also the *most loved* son. It may seem like I am repeating myself, but it is a different concept. The relationship between Jacob and Joseph went beyond mere acceptance and favor. It transcended status or place in the family order. Jacob loved Joseph with genuine heartfelt feeling.

For many of you who have been exposed to the Bible for years, the thought that God loves you is nothing new. We've all read John 3:16. He gave His Son because He loved...me.

In this amazing story from Genesis, the Father wants us to see the deep and abiding affection that God feels toward each of us. Sometimes our hearts and minds become callous, and we miss the deep, personal things coming from the Father-heart of God. But don't miss this: God has genuine affection and heartfelt feelings for you! It's true! He even *likes* you!

In the Old Testament, God is described as one

who sings over you as a parent would sing over his own child, the child that is flesh of his flesh and bone of his bone. The Bible says the heart of God loves you and rejoices over you as a child in whom He has great delight.

Let the Holy Spirit help you understand this wonderful truth. Only when we have genuinely experienced God's favor and affection can we trust His dreams for us. We begin, for the first time, to open the door to partnering with Him. We realize that we will find our true life in the places He has for us to go, the things He has for us to do, the people He has for us to meet.

> *Only when we have genuinely experienced God's favor and affection can we trust His dreams for us.*

NURTURING OTHERS

Some years ago, Robert Manley, a newspaper publisher in a small Massachusetts town, left for England. Nothing unusual about that, except Manley left in a thirteen-and-one-half foot sailboat. He'd always wanted to cross the Atlantic by boat, and he decided to try it. I mention this adventure because I've always cherished the response of two people in this man's life. Manley's wife encouraged him to follow his dream, but it was what she didn't say that meant the most to him: She never brought up death or trouble, or asked who was going to take care of this or that while he was away. Manley's sister simply gave him a short note: "Go ahead and do it! You ought to try. It's tragic so few of us ever attempt our dreams."

Weeks later, as he neared the little port town where his journey would end, he saw a crowd of hundreds lining the waterfront. As he approached the dock, his eyes scanned the crowd until he saw his wife standing just slightly apart from everyone else. She had wanted him to pursue his dream, and she was there for him at the end when his dream was realized.

How can we be the kind of people who give others the environment they need to dream? How can we create for others—and ourselves—that place of acceptance, affection, and support that sets us free to become all God intended?

When was the last time you said to a dreamer: *"You can do it!"*

In my experience, God is extraordinarily open and trusting with us as we move toward our dream. He rarely intervenes in our decision-making process. More often, He chooses to help or redirect—always ready to step in with His wonderful redemption. Even when we wander off track, God works in mysterious ways to guide the paths of those who trust in Him, those who "lean not to their own understanding."

Our Father reveals to each of us His gentle heart. In the Psalms, David exclaims, "Thy right hand upholds me; and Thy gentleness makes me great" (Psalm 18:35). God invites us to nurture the dreams of others in the same manner.

TO TRUST AGAIN

Later in our story about Joseph, Jacob sent him to check on his brothers. He told him to go to Shechem and find out what was going on there. He asked Joseph to bring back word of everything his brothers were saying and doing, and he trusted Joseph to do as he had asked. The interesting thing about the timing of Jacob's request is that it came on the heels of a rebuke he had just given his son. In spite of Joseph's mistakes and failures, Jacob trusted him with an assignment.

It is a powerful lesson about how God views His children. This kind of trusting environment is rare, even in the church. Make a mistake, and you will be forgiven. You can still stick around. You'll even be loved. But make a mistake, and you won't be asked to do anything. There's always a limit to our forgiveness and acceptance.

Jesus comes to Peter after his miserable failure asking, "Do you love me?" Each time Peter says, "Yes," Jesus makes a request: "Feed my sheep." Now, there's a God who nurtures the heart of the dreamer.

An environment of trust makes vision and hope possible; it helps you believe in your personal significance. If you're like me, you've found yourself saying something like, *I've done some things this week…and if I were God I wouldn't trust me.* But He does. He's ready to trust you with an assignment. He has a calling for your life.

AGAINST GREAT ODDS

Joseph lived in a hostile environment. It is one thing to begin to grasp that you are favored, that you are loved, that you are trusted. But you also need to come to grips with the reality that there are people who won't like you. Please hear me. It's good that you know you're in this place of grace where you are favored, where you're loved, and where you're trusted, but don't delude yourself into thinking that it will be smooth sailing.

Some people will deny the possibility that your dream could ever happen. They will look you in the eye and say very convincingly, "No way!" At those times, you can stand steady and rejoice because tension can bring even greater clarity to the dream. God can use opposition to knock off the rough edges, to keep your goal from getting blurred.

However, we never serve others well if we say to them, "You can do it—no problem." Better to say, "You can do it—but there will be problems and we can work through them." God never says, "No problem." God says, "You can face all the problems that will come, through Christ Jesus who strengthens you." The very fact that God says He will strengthen you is a clue that you'll be tested.

You may have personal dreams of restoration for your home and marriage, dreams for your business, perhaps a dream to be in ministry. The Lord wants to restore your God-given privilege to call yourself a dreamer.

Even if you feel disqualified in certain ways for the dream, God can make it possible for you through Jesus Christ. Even though you find yourself in a hostile environment with enemies bent on thwarting you, God will never forsake the dream He Himself is summoning forth in your soul.

In Jesus Christ, He's made possible this favored place—He's made possible a dream. And because of Jesus Christ, the door has been opened for God to lavish His affection upon you. You have things to be and things to do that have had your name written on them for eternity.

GOD, I TRUST YOU WITH MY LIFE

Lord Jesus, You are up to something in my world, and I want to be a part of it. I trust You, Lord.

How blessed I am to dwell in the favored place of Your special affection. Thank You that I am "accepted in the Beloved." Accepted in You.

Prepare me to receive the assignment; the calling You have for my life through the power of Your Holy Spirit. Amen.

PART TWO

Preparing
for Promise

3
BROKEN TO HIS LIKENESS

In your moment of brokenness, Jesus asks "Do you love me?"

Every child of God lives in a state of tension, of waiting, and of longing. Something is happening inside you—something beyond your control. In your spirit, you sense that you're in motion, you're on your way somewhere—and even though you're not quite there yet, you want it oh, so desperately.

The Apostle Paul describes this state of tension as an "inward groaning"—in fact, he said all creation groans with us, like a woman in the pangs of childbirth.

What we are describing is a birthing process. You are in the process of being remade from the inside out.

Simply put, God is making each of us over, making us new so that we look like Someone else. We are being "conformed to the likeness of his Son, that he (Jesus) might be the firstborn among many brothers" (Romans 8:29, NIV). When the Father, the Son, and the Holy Spirit first said, "Let us make man in our image," their intention was to create a human race that would share a beautiful and single family likeness.

And God's creative plan has never changed.

Right now, at this very moment, your process of *becoming* is in motion. God is always at work. Little, insignificant things, or large, all-consuming things—each one is being used by Him to make you more like Jesus. What you experience as a difficult situation or a challenging relationship, God wants to use to conform you into the image of His Son—so that Jesus Christ can be the firstborn among many.

God is up to something in your life:

> He wants to remake you in His likeness so that He can accomplish your true destiny by the power and authority that comes from His nature.

Imagine a man who has been so conformed to Jesus' image that just by knowing him the people he comes in contact with every day—his wife, his children, men and women at work—discover God and their own individual potential.

Imagine a woman who, by her relationship with God through Jesus Christ, is released to become the person she was originally designed to be. She has no need to contend for her rights. She already has authority—she mirrors the Person of Christ. And every life she touches is changed for the better.

This man and woman demonstrate God's plan as

set from the beginning. His calling on our lives is to live out Jesus Christ's likeness and power in our world. It is our destiny. It's what all the waiting and groaning are about. It's where we are headed—if we will let God's remaking process go on to completion in our lives.

THE PROCESS OF BECOMING

In this wonderful process of becoming like Jesus, God accomplishes His plans for each of us in three primary ways. I describe them as the *making,* the *shaping,* and the *breaking* of the man or woman of God.

The principal tool in the *making* is God's call or assignment for you—whatever task He has placed in your life. It is God's gift and purpose for you. Think of Joseph or David or of Mary, the mother of Jesus. Their unique lives grew out of their unique callings.

God always gives us something to do that we can't accomplish on our own. It's always just slightly beyond the reach of our human skills. Yet embracing this impossible destiny is the first step in becoming like Christ.

After you have accepted God's invitation, His *shaping* of you begins. The Word of God is the principal tool He uses to direct and define your life so that you are equipped for accomplishing the assignment God has given you. When I say the Word, I'm not only referring to the Bible, but also to God's daily voice in your life. This eternal and personal—and very dynamic—Word of God brings definition and motivation to your decisions.

Ask, "What has God been saying to me in the last two weeks?" You're His chosen child, and you've responded to His high mission for your life—why wouldn't He be in nearly constant conversation with you? If you can't identify a personal word that God has been using to penetrate your defenses; if you can't think of any affirming, confirming, or confronting work of God in your life, then you're not being shaped. Let me assure you that when God speaks to you, you will know it. And let me further assure you that the Lord is faithful to speak.

When He speaks, our privilege is to respond to His shaping touch:

He speaks, He prompts, He presses, He pleads.

We hear, we respond, we follow, we exclaim, "Yes, Lord!"

Through this tender yet powerful dynamic, our life takes on a different look. We become more like Christ. God is leading us to our destiny. He is at work transforming our very being.

The third way that God changes us is through *breaking,* a process that's often misunderstood. Of course, it sounds pretty negative: "I love you so much

I'm going to break you!" Not exactly something you'd go looking for.

But God's way of breaking is different from the pain, destruction, or waste that first comes to mind when we think about breaking. What does it mean to be broken in God's economy? God's way of breaking corrects, adjusts, releases. It allows for new life to invade our routines—and for us to escape our hard-shelled, impoverished existence. God's way of breaking is not intended to hurt—although we will probably experience pain. God's intention through breaking is for healing, redeeming, freedom, and newness of life.

In all my years of ministry, I've never met a man or a woman who is becoming like Jesus Christ who has not been, or is not being, broken.

> *God's way of breaking is not intended to hurt—*
> *although we may experience pain.*
> *God's intention through breaking is for healing,*
> *redeeming, freedom, and newness of life.*

Consider the big picture: You understand the call God has placed on your life. You begin to move toward your destiny. As you do, God begins shaping you as you listen for and heed His voice. But now that you have committed yourself to God's agenda, you are also vulnerable to it. Remember that His whole purpose is to conform you to the image of His Son. But I must tell you that once you sign on to God's purpose, you will be broken.

Why? Every single one of us has something in us that cannot be healed. It has to be broken. Whatever this "something" in you is, you can't be delivered from it, healed of it, or empowered to resist it. This something in us is what philosophers call the sin of hubris. Greeks understood hubris to be ambitious pride in one's own goodness that scorns any higher divine moral order. You see, a man's hubris isn't an ambition for evil but for good. Hubris is unfailingly sincere and well intentioned. Hubris has all the outward marks of righteousness and goodness—and a heart of utter arrogance.

And that's the terrible thing. Hubris is the deadliest kind of pride because it first appears to be goodness. In the act of trying so diligently to be and do good—to say, "I'm going to be like Jesus"—hubris becomes the ultimate lie.

It takes the *life of Jesus* to live the life of Jesus. We lie to ourselves and others when we strive for righteousness in our own strength when we are merely human. No matter how hard we try, or how much goodness or energy or skill we bring to the effort, we'll never pull it off. But, oh, how we like to try.

CAUGHT IN LOVE

The man in the Scriptures who best illustrates the sin of hubris is Simon Peter. He is like us, making all the commitments and confessions that make us proud to be members of the human race. Peter is absolutely sincere, completely genuine, without guile. His motives are pure. His insights are stunning. When he declares, "Lord, You're the only one who has the words of life," we know he's seen the light while the rest of the disciples are still in the dark. Alone, he knows that Jesus is the Son of the Living God. Later when he says, "They may do that, but I never will!" we believe him completely.

And why shouldn't we? Peter is as good as it gets. That's why we're just as stunned as Peter when Jesus says to this prince of a man, "You're going to betray me three times."

Jesus goes on to say, "Satan has demanded permission to sift you like wheat; but I have prayed for you, that your faith may not fail" (Luke 22:31–32). Clearly, Jesus knows a breaking will come for Peter—and He allows it.

How easy it is to trust God to a point—then balk when we realize He may allow Satan to test us. But Jesus Christ, who is no respecter of persons, will let every one of His loved ones go through seasons of testing. The same dazzling and terrible disease of hubris that affected Peter—"I can pull it off—the rest of them can't, but watch me!"—infects us too.

A number of years ago, startling revelations of sexual immorality and financial scandals came out in the newspapers about several of our better-known media evangelists. Many of us said, "I've made my mistakes, but I would *never* do that!" But the proper response when we're confronted with one who has failed Jesus Christ utterly is to admit, "I could do that too."

Live with the discomfort of those words. Struggle with the simple ugliness of them. Because what was in Peter is in you. You cannot be like Jesus Christ without the life of Jesus Christ. Better to come to the place where you confess, "I don't want to fail like that, Lord. But if I don't have You, I will fail."

The deep transformation into God's likeness doesn't begin and end here. God will let Satan have access to your life—so that you can discover it is impossible to carry out your promises without His power. Yet the principal tool in the breaking of a man or woman of God is not his or her failure or sin, or even any terrible circumstance that might befall. For a clue to what I mean, let's look closely at the conversation Peter had with the Lord after he denied ever knowing Jesus.

After His death and resurrection, Jesus began making appearances throughout Jerusalem and the

Galilee region. In fact, He was with Peter twice without bringing up that dark, dark night when Peter horribly failed the Lord. This silence on the part of Jesus led Peter deeper into his own discouragement and sense of failure.

Peter finally concluded that he would never be able to follow Jesus and decided to return to what he knew best—fishing. Peter persuaded a few of his buddies to go along and set off for the Sea of Galilee. Of course, we discover in John 21 that the very thing he felt confident enough to do, he couldn't do either. All night long Peter fished—and came up with nothing.

At dawn, a voice came over the water, "Throw the net on the other side!" You can almost hear Peter grumbling, "Somebody's *always* telling me what to do!"

Reluctantly, he hauled in the net and threw it over the other side. John records that the net filled with 153 big fish. Not sardines—big fish! Maybe that's when John started studying the shoreline to find out the identity of the mystery fishing guide. Soon he jabbed Peter in the ribs. "It's the Lord!" he blurted out.

Peter looked at the figure walking on the beach, then jumped into the water and started swimming to shore. When the boat pulled in, he singlehandedly dragged the bulging net ashore. I imagine that under the surface of all Peter's hyperactivity was guilt, terrible frustration, and an enormous desire to restore himself in the eyes of Jesus. Yet when he finally hauled in the catch and stood on the beach dripping wet and exhausted, Peter discovered that the Lord *already had* fish—and was preparing him breakfast.

There, in the presence of Jesus, the remarkable conversation began. "Peter, do you love Me?"

I sense Peter thinking, *Good, an easy one!* "Yes," he said to Jesus.

A dramatic pause. Then Jesus asked again, simply and gently, "Peter, do you love me?"

I imagine Peter thinking, *Did I miss something?* Possibly a quiet rage began to build. *Okay, I blew it,* he thought, trying to swallow his punishment. *I deserve this. Here it comes. Let's just get it over with.*

And Jesus asked the third time, "Peter, do you truly love me?"

Then it all came apart in Peter. "Lord, you know everything! You know where 153 big fish are! You know I love you! You know I've failed."

Only then could Jesus give back to Peter His purpose in life. "Peter, follow me. Love my lambs. Feed my sheep."

Can you see it? Word by word, glance by glance, Jesus is making, shaping, and breaking Peter. Right before our eyes, we see our loving Lord at work. Jesus, the Author and Finisher of our faith, lovingly took a proud, foolish, sincere Peter (so much like us, don't you think?) and brought him a huge step closer to Jesus' own beautiful likeness.

THE SAVIOR WHO INTERVENES

Think with me now about the tool God used in the breaking of Peter—and uses as well in us. It's not His love for us that breaks our heart, though that is a compelling part of our relationship with the Lord. What breaks your heart and mine is being forced to recognize that even though we have failed Him miserably, we genuinely do love Him. *We love Him desperately, and we can't pull it off without Him.*

Colliding with this truth is what breaks the sin of hubris. We have failed Him—only to discover that He doesn't want to talk about our failures. He wants to talk about our love.

We're taught that if we really love, we won't do certain things. Or if we do certain things, then we don't really love. "You told me you loved me," a forlorn daughter wails to her father, "but that must not be true because you left!"

"You made a commitment to me," a man tells his estranged wife, "but that love and that affection can't be genuine because if it were genuine, you wouldn't have done that."

That's how we think. When loyalty is breached,

when failure occurs, we automatically take away all of the value that might be there. We say that the two can't possibly coexist—failure and love together.

But they can. It's possible to terribly deny the Lord and still deeply love the Savior. That's what makes men and women weep bitter tears. In our brush with sin and death, we have discovered our mortality. We finally have accepted the truth that no matter how honest and good our commitments are, we don't have the strength to pull them off alone.

> *We have failed Him—only to discover*
> *that He doesn't want to talk about our failures.*
> *He wants to talk about our love.*

In your moment of brokenness, Jesus sets the stage to intervene in your life, to give you the chance in the face of your failure to say, "I do love You, Lord." Only Jesus can do this, just as He did with Peter. Only He can put you back on the road of living the life God intended. He comes to you in these moments of failure as you confess your love, and says to you, as He did to Peter, "All right, then. I want you to do something important. Even though you failed me, you say you love Me. I believe you. So here's an assignment."

Wherever you are in the making, the shaping, or the breaking process, you are headed toward His likeness. He desires that you not only arrive at your full potential but are in a position to release others around you to reach their potential as well. Of course, there are no shortcuts in this remaking journey. And birthing always involves pain.

But there needn't be any uncertainty either. Until the day when you see Jesus face to face, your faithful God will be conforming you—calling you to His very likeness.

LORD, MAKE ME LIKE YOU

Lord Jesus, thank You for Your mercy that keeps me from getting what I deserve. Thank You for Your grace that helps me experience what I can never earn.

When I fail You, thank You for speaking words of love and acceptance to me, Jesus. May the truth of Your calling and purpose in my life grow brighter with each passing day. Amen.

4
WRESTLING WITH GOD

There's nothing more difficult than giving up to God—yet it is in surrender that we find our destiny.

A while back, I spent some time with a man in our church who had buried his wife several years before. I had never had the opportunity to hear him talk about what it was like to see her struggle with her cancer, and I asked him to tell me something about the story.

He told me how he had nursed her, cared for her, bathed her. He talked about how she never once lost her composure, even in times of great pain. As I listened to him pour out his heart, I felt like crying. But in the middle of the story, I sensed the Lord speaking to me. "This man has something you don't have," He said.

And my honest, quick response was, "Whatever it is, I don't want it."

Men and women who have gone through incredibly difficult times in life have wrestled through important issues. In the process, they have made quiet decisions that few people ever know about—and a mark is left on their lives. For us, it might appear to be a mark of suffering—and our first response is to turn away—but for them it's not.

In the struggle, they've discovered some things about God and themselves that set them apart, that sanctify them. They no longer struggle with some of the things that you and I still struggle with. Certain issues have been settled.

The life of Jacob can teach us a great deal about the mystery of this sanctifying work in our lives. Jacob understood little about God's ways until he was a grown man. He spent much of his life manipulating and lying and scheming to get his own way. He thought that the end justified the means. And the end he wanted was a good one—the destiny God had promised him. He just wasn't overly concerned about how he got it.

How did this selfish, manipulative man become the man after whom the whole nation of God's chosen people was named? More to the point for us, how can we become men and women who are willing to surrender our way to His? How can we secure the blessing that allows us to fulfill God's original intention for our lives? Seeing how Jacob the schemer became Israel, a man of God, will shed light on our path as we, too, seek to understand God's ways in our life.

Our story begins with the words of God Himself spoken over the two boys who occupied the womb of Rebekah, the beloved wife of Isaac. Speaking words of promise and destiny, God revealed to her that Jacob, the younger son, would rule over the older son, Esau, and that from his line a chosen nation would come (Genesis 25:23). You could say that Jacob had a canopy above him and a foundation beneath him from the moment of his birth. The canopy and the foundation were God's divine decree.

Early on, however, it became apparent that Jacob was going to grab what had been promised instead of letting God fulfill His word in His own time and in His own way. First, he tricked his older brother, Esau, into selling the birthright of the firstborn. Then he stole Esau's blessing from his father, Isaac. To escape the family's anger after his deceit, Jacob had to flee. Leaving his family, his people, and his heritage four hundred miles behind, Jacob journeyed to a strange land.

Over the next twenty years, the God of his father, Isaac, spoke to him twice. The first occurrence was shortly after he fled his homeland. God said something like this: "Even though you're an idiot, I'm still who I am, and I'm not going to leave you. In fact, I'm going to take care of you and bless you even though you're going to work real hard at messing up your life!"

Jacob's response was predictably self-centered: "Well, if you're really God and You do manage to take care of me, then I'll let You be my God." Such a deal Jacob offered God! It's no wonder he didn't hear from God again for twenty years.

Meanwhile, Jacob became a very prosperous man. Of course, he thought that he was prosperous because he was Jacob. Most of us think that way. But God was faithful, protecting Jacob through a number of schemes, and blessing him even as Jacob tried to outwit everyone around him.

After twenty years, God spoke a second time. "Jacob, if you want to get on with your life," God told him, "you're going to have to go backward. I'm asking you to go back to your family, to the land you left behind."

Despite his previous failures, Jacob was obedient. He agreed to go back. It is on Jacob's journey home that we witness one of the most famous stories in all of the Old Testament—the wrestling match between Jacob and God. It's a great story, rich in insight for our own lives.

A HEART PREPARED

Along the way home, Jacob showed signs of progress in three separate incidents that prepared him for God to work in his life. The years of distance and separation had been used by God to soften the soil of Jacob's heart, to set the stage for the move of God's Spirit when the time was right. First, when Uncle Laban chased him down to try to bring him back, Jacob showed his determination to follow God's leading.

Whatever Laban could offer if Jacob returned, whatever unknowns might lie ahead, Jacob decided to obey. So too in our lives God invites us to follow Him. But at some moment it will always involve our determination to obey—to change our direction.

Later in the journey Jacob stopped to make camp, and he realized that angels were camped there too. He called this place *Mahansim,* the Hebrew word for "two camps" or "double camp." Through this little incident, Jacob understood that there are two dimensions, or "camps," to life—the physical and the spiritual. Jacob finally saw that God was there with him in "both camps." He came to the place where he finally acknowledged that God was with him *right where he was.*

What a helpful insight for us! Wherever you are right now, God is there. You may be running *from* God or running *to* Him. Either way, God has plans for your life, a purpose from which He has not deviated. I promise you that wherever you're camping, God is camped there too.

In the final scene prior to God's ultimate confrontation with Jacob, Jacob battled terror. He was about to encounter his betrayed brother, Esau. When his messengers returned to report that Esau was approaching with four hundred warriors, Jacob knew he was in trouble! After all, he had never reconciled with his brother since he had cheated him out of his inheritance twenty years earlier. He knew there was unfinished business.

What did Jacob do? First he divided his caravan into two companies and sent one on ahead bearing lavish gifts. "At least," he figured, "if half of us are destroyed, the other half can escape." And then came the most interesting tactic of all—Jacob prayed. This was new behavior for the schemer.

It was a long, fearful, self-serving prayer. Actually, it was rather comical—Jacob felt the need to remind God of His recent promises to protect him (in case God had already forgotten!). But don't miss the point—at this moment of great testing, Jacob prayed. God doesn't care much about the greatness of our prayers. When you come to a great moment of testing, just pray!

> *When you come to a great moment of testing, just pray!*

These three, seemingly insignificant events that occurred as Jacob journeyed back to the land of his father set the stage for Jacob's life-changing encounter with God. His determination to obey, his humble acknowledgment of God's presence, and his simple, yet heartfelt prayer, positioned him to do business with God when He showed up along the River Jabbok. The stage was set for a gripping moment in the life of this man who was so much like us.

STRUGGLE IN THE DARK

Now Jacob was drawing near to his moment of reckoning. The Bible tells us that he had sent everyone across the river ahead of him. Let's follow the biblical narrative:

> He arose that night and took his two wives, his two maidservants, and his eleven sons, and crossed over the ford of Jabbok. He took them, sent them over the brook, and sent over what he had. Then Jacob was left alone; and a Man wrestled with him until the breaking of day. Now when He saw that He did not prevail against him, He touched the socket of his hip; and the socket of Jacob's hip was out of joint as He wrestled with him. And He said, "Let me go, for the day breaks."
>
> But he said, "I will not let You go unless You bless me!"
>
> So He said to him, "What is your name?"
> And he said, "Jacob."
> And He said, "Your name shall no longer be called Jacob, but Israel; for you have struggled with God and with men, and have prevailed."...
> And He blessed him there.
>
> And Jacob called the name of the place Peniel: "For I have seen God face to face, and

my life is preserved" (Genesis 32:22–30, NKJV).

Something happened to Jacob in those hours of contest.

First, notice that Jacob was alone at night. He experienced what is often referred to as the "dark night of the soul." Pastor Jack Hayford talks about "tomb time." No life stirring. Everything's dead.

The night speaks of no light, of not hearing anything, of not seeing anything, of not being able to tell what's going on. It's a fearful, confusing time. But in those times, when you're all alone in the dark, important things get decided.

When we come together in fellowship, whether in a church setting or maybe even one on one with another believer, we make significant responses that impact our daily lives. But while the truly important themes of life may be confirmed during our times together, that's not where they are decided. Decision happens when there's no one else around, when you're wrestling through the stuff of your life alone with God. It was that way for Abraham. Alone and at night, God came to him. It was that way for Moses, David, Isaiah, Daniel—even for Jesus as He agonized alone with the Father in the Garden.

At those times, when you're wrestling it through

with God, you make choices about integrity and surrender that will change the rest of your life.

The second thing to observe about Jacob's encounter with God is the crippling effect it had on Jacob. "Just as he crossed over Penuel the sun rose on him, and he limped on his hip…because He touched the socket of Jacob's hip in the muscle that shrank" (Genesis 32:31–32).

I confess it bothers me that God would "touch" a man so that he limps the rest of his life. Not only do I not like that idea, I don't want it to happen to me. Yet I've come to understand that even though God will occasionally cripple someone, that "touch" is not a mark of defeat. A moment of crippling from God is really a moment of crowning—when a person has a distinguishing mark placed on his or her life.

As Jacob limps away from the scene of his struggle, he is to all outward appearances a cripple—a defeated man. But the man is now more whole than he has ever been in his life. Though he limps, his heart surges with a certainty he has never possessed before this moment.

VICTORY IN SURRENDER

Let's not forget that Jacob wins the wrestling match. When the Man says to Jacob, "You have prevailed with men," God is not vindicating or validating all the years of Jacob's scheming. Rather, He's affirming that Jacob has changed directions. He's recognizing that he prevailed with Laban. He did not allow the counsel of a schemer to divert him from his course. God says, "I asked you to go back, and you've come back. You didn't let anything keep you from that. You have prevailed with men."

What does Scripture mean, then, when it says that Jacob also "prevailed with God"? Do you think that Jacob actually pinned the angel? One, two, three, you're out! I don't think so. Jacob finally "wins" in this way: At the moment when all of his skill, strength, and resolve are matched up against the Man from God, *Jacob realizes that he wants what God has to offer more than everything he can get or become on his own.* God allows all of Jacob's powers of manipulation to be concentrated into one moment, to be played out before his eyes. In that moment, Jacob realizes that hanging on with everything he has is not enough. He bursts out, "I cannot let you go until you bless me!"

We might mistake Jacob's request as an insatiable desire for more. Yet in this moment of conflict, Jacob simply understands that his wives, his children, his herds, all of his possessions amount to nothing if he cannot have the blessing of this One who represents infinite wealth. He prevails with God because he sees what God can offer and he chooses that over what he can get on his own.

It's a decision each of us must make. We can choose to run away thinking that life and good times will go on forever. Or we can acknowledge God's call and surrender to life as He originally intended. We can step into the promise that is ours as a child of destiny.

If you want something finer, something that God has ordained for eternity, then, like Jacob, you'll come to a moment of choice, of struggle. In that moment you will know that it's going to take every bit of strength you have to surrender. Why? Because every fiber of your nature and every shred of personal experience has trained you to scheme, strain, and struggle to the very end to survive as an independent human being. Your human nature tells you, "We either win this one, or we're dead!"

There's nothing more difficult than giving up to God. But if you'll make that decision in a moment of aloneness with God, something will be settled. You'll be different. You will receive *the mark of surrender.* Things will never be quite the same. *You* will never be quite the same.

Through the pages of Scripture we get to witness this great moment between God and Jacob. Jacob defaults to the higher standard. He surrenders—not to death, but to life. And that is why he wins.

> *Every fiber of your nature and every shred*
> *of personal experience has trained you*
> *to scheme, strain, and struggle.*

A NEW NAME

In this moment of surrender, God does a surprising thing—He gives Jacob a new name. God says to him, "Your name was Jacob." Jacob means *supplanter.* "From now on you will be called Israel." Israel means, *Struggles with, or rules with, God.* Jacob, who has been governed by his own will now is ruled by God. He did not win by superior strength but by the superiority that comes through surrender.

Jacob was marked by God. He carried the effects of that moment of encounter for the rest of his life. But God also spoke a word of promise into his life in that moment of surrender. A word of hope and destiny. A word that identified the new man that Jacob had become.

God wants to give you a new name. A name that reflects the work He has done in your life. As you surrender to Him, He'll call you something that you never would have been called otherwise. Are you a people-pleaser? God will give you new courage to make decisions of integrity. Is your lifelong struggle with fear? With some weakness in your character? God will call you "Peaceful" or "Strong." He wants new dimensions of His mind, His Spirit, His nature to flow through your life. You will discover, just as Jacob discovers from this time on, that there's a whole new way of walking, a whole new way of living. No longer the manipulator, Jacob becomes a man of faith who leads his people into their future as the chosen race. In his surrender, he finds his destiny.

True surrender flows out of an important moment of contest when you are challenged. You finally see that He is infinitely better and infinitely stronger than who you are or what you have. And though it takes everything you are, you give up. What feels like the end, is really your place of beginning.

LORD OF STRIVERS, CALL MY NAME

Lord Jesus, I invite You to enter into conflict with me so that I may learn the joy of surrender. I long for a new name, a name of Your choosing.

Calm my fears. Fill me with courage by Your Spirit. I want to do the hard work of letting go, into Your loving hands, all that is less than Your best.

In Your strong name, Amen.

5
GOD'S COMMITMENT TO REALITY

If we refuse to face our painful realities, we will never experience the One who comes to nurture, heal, and strengthen.

One of my dearest friends had cancer invading his body. Throughout the ordeal, he was pretty straight with me about things like blood count and medication. He told me about promises that the Lord had given him. But even though we shared fairly openly about it all, every now and then a kind of fuzziness crept into our conversations that I had a hard time identifying.

You've experienced what I'm talking about. You ask someone, "How's it going?"

They say, "Fine, wonderful."

Fuzzy.

You know it's not fine and it's not wonderful, but they want to say it is because that response makes them feel better, or maybe they just don't want to talk about painful facts.

My conversations with my buddy were this way. He tried to be honest. But when we talked about prognosis, when I tried to pin him down on what the doctors were really saying, he turned vague. He'd change the subject, or use some trite phrase in response, or back out of the conversation altogether.

Then the doctors called him in for a conference. They told him he had come to a significant crossroad in terms of the cancer's development. For the first time, my friend allowed his wife to sit down with him and the doctor.

It was interesting to me how much clearer the picture became after that meeting. His wife's loving, concerned, and very pointed questions broke through all the fuzziness. Now they knew exactly what would happen next, what medical steps would need to be faced, and how long he had to live. All the issues that he was having so much trouble facing on his own suddenly got pinned down and defined. The next time we talked, the vagueness was gone. My friend had a clear and meaningful grasp of reality.

How prone each of us is to want to escape reality! We go to great lengths to alter the facts or to adjust them in our minds so that we live in emotional comfort. It seems better than coming to grips with *where* we really are or *who* we really are.

Sometimes it strikes me that humans are like deer on the run before a pack of wolves. Think of the wolves as unpleasant realities that we feel we must avoid in order to have the life we want. We could quite easily name each wolf—pain, effort, shame, fear, ignorance, habit—but the reason we're on the run usually boils down to one simple truth; we don't want to get hurt.

I know you could describe some of the ways this run from reality plays out in our lives: We work too much, eat too much, play too much. We try to make money without working. We escape into video games, romance novels, or movies. In our relationships, we can evade our responsibility for years, never working through problems, and never arriving at the life God originally intended. For example, husbands and wives can create a fantasy world of sex because their physical relationship with their spouse is so ordinary.

Does any of this surprise you? Not me. Reality can be a tough scene.

THE GREAT INVASION

As determined as we are to escape or adjust reality, we can easily overlook how much God is committed to reality! In fact, He invaded *our reality.* He came to dwell on earth among men. That's what the Incarnation is all about: the unbelievable *reality* that God became man. Jesus Christ emptied Himself of His divinity that He might become a human being like you and me. It is in the Incarnation that we see first-hand God's commitment to reality.

Paul describes the strength of God's commitment:

Let this mind be in you, which was also in Christ Jesus: Who, being in the form of God, thought it not robbery to be equal with God: But made himself of no reputation, and took upon him the form of a servant, and was made in the likeness of men: And being found in fashion as a man, he humbled himself, and became obedient unto death, even the death of the cross.

Wherefore God also hath highly exalted him, and given him a name which is above every name: That at the name of Jesus every knee should bow, of things in heaven, and things in earth, and things under the earth; and that every tongue should confess that Jesus Christ is Lord, to the glory of God the Father. (Philippians 2:5–11, KJV)

Jesus Christ knew who He was, the Son of the Living God. Yet He let go of His identity and became like us, entering the darkness of our world. His birth didn't take place in the heavenlies. Although the plan had its origin before time began (1 Corinthians 2:7), at the moment of its manifestation it happened in our world, not in some other reality.

Do you want to encounter the Christian God? Then listen for a baby's cry. Reach out and touch Him—that's a feed crib He's sleeping in. Smell the hay.

Hear the animals stirring in the barn. Feel the restlessness of the crowds outside in the streets who were summoned to Bethlehem for a census.

Welcome to the world Jesus was born into. Our world. We don't have a mystical religion in a fantasy world. God invaded the messy reality of this planet so that He could bring the reality of His light into our darkness. In His process of calling us to freedom, God is committed to reality.

> *God invaded the messy reality of this planet so that He could bring the reality of His light into our darkness. God is committed to reality.*

We have trouble with reality. The darkness of our world can be frightening or confusing. The last thing we want to do is face the way things really are or the way we are. It's easier just to pretend. Or hide. We're really good at that. We've actually been hiding ever since Adam and Eve had their first encounters with God. And in the Garden of Eden we get our first clues about God's commitment to reality.

WHERE ARE YOU HIDING?

After Adam sinned, God came looking for him in the cool of the evening. "Adam, where are you?" the Creator asked.

Where are you? That's a surprising question. God knew exactly where Adam was—hiding behind the third bush on the left. Adam was doing what fallen man intuitively does when he sins—he was adjusting reality.

When things aren't going right, when we're up against a difficult situation, when we discover some dark spot in our character or personality, when we're face to face with someone we can't get along with or who's disappointed us, we want to adjust reality. We will do anything we can to hide, to cover up, to blame. Our reaction is like breathing for us—it's our nature. And it's at precisely these moments that God's commitment to reality is clearest!

The problem was not that God couldn't find Adam. It was that Adam didn't realize he was hiding. The point of God's question was to help Adam see the truth.

Do you know where you are? Being out of harmony with God in any area of your life forces you to hide. And to the degree you succeed in hiding, to whatever degree you succeed in adjusting reality, to that degree you avoid the Savior. God may not show up with the exact question, "Where are you?" But He'll begin to arrange the circumstances of your life until there isn't one more bush for you to hide behind. One way or another, He'll confront you with the reality of who you are and where you are.

Our Savior does not offer a salvation that makes it possible for us to escape the reality of a corrupt world. Frankly, this is disappointing to some—and it's the starting point for countless cults and psychological scams that promise to deliver something more appealing.

A more troubling fact to me is that, because we're so highly skilled at avoiding reality in any area that matters (marriage, parenting, business, personal integrity), we can easily avoid the salvation our Savior offers. Imagine a child who wanders away from his mother in the supermarket—he's scared, so he hides. He doesn't realize that now it's much harder for Mommy to "save" him. In the same way, we can run away from the very salvation that we so desperately need and want.

When this happens, not only do we lose out, but those around us do too. Think about your relationships—with your spouse, your parents, your children, your boss. Who you are and what you do has an extraordinary shaping influence on the lives of others. Yet when we're having conflict in a relationship, it's extremely difficult to face the darkness within ourselves that might be contributing to the conflict. When we manage to lay the blame on others and avoid dealing with the reality of our own fallenness, we run away from God's healing and saving light.

If we want God's light, we'll eventually have to face the darkness of our own heart and mind—in whatever area it exists. Light can only shine in the darkness. This is God's way, and it shows His commitment to reality. How do I know this? Because Jesus Christ Himself, the Light of the World, came into darkness. Jesus faced the terrible darkness of the reality of our world—and invaded it with His light.

THE HOPE OF REALITY

For a compelling portrait of our world's darkness, read the Books of Isaiah, Jeremiah, and Ezekiel. They tell the story of how the Jewish people went their own way, lacked commitment to God, and reveled in their sin. God's own people refused to seek God because they didn't trust Him. Nothing much has changed in three thousand years.

The unhappy role of the prophets was to declare the consequences of such behavior—the coming destruction of Jerusalem, for example, and the captivity that would follow. Yet remarkably, in all of the warnings of doom and destruction that fill the prophetic books, a promise of blessing always breaks through. It keeps showing up—a thread of hope that something better is coming, even in the face of the darkness.

Isaiah, for example, spoke to his people about a

new king who would come from their royal line. This new kind of king would be a man of power and wisdom. His name was King Hezekiah, and he would bring great revival to Judah and to Jerusalem.

And Isaiah saw something more, something beyond. He began to prophesy about a coming Savior, the King of kings, the Son of God. Isaiah not only saw deeply into the present, he also saw dramatically into the future. A promised king was coming and behind him the promised Messiah. Both would bring revival. Both would bring renewal. And both would offer salvation.

Isaiah was caught between two worlds. He could see the truth of what was happening in his own culture, yet he also had the spiritual vision to see that something was coming for all the world. He saw both the immediate and the eternal. He saw both the hard realities of *now*, and the hopeful realities of tomorrow that make life bearable.

For unto us a child is born, unto us a son is given: and the government will be upon his shoulder: and his name shall be called Wonderful, Counsellor, The mighty God, The everlasting Father, The Prince of Peace. Of the increase of his government and peace there shall be no end, upon the throne of David, and upon his kingdom, to order it, and to establish it with judgment and with justice from henceforth even for ever. The zeal of the LORD of hosts will perform this. (Isaiah 9:6–7, KJV)

Light shines forth in darkness. That's what Isaiah prophesied. That's what actually happened. The Light shone forth in the darkness. In the reality of darkness, light revealed a reason to hope. After all, we don't need a Savior unless we suffer from sin. We never need redemption unless we're in bondage. We don't need a liberator unless we're oppressed.

If we refuse to own our painful truths and embrace our own suffering, we will never experience the Succoring One—the One who comes to nurture, heal, and strengthen. If we deny that we are in darkness, we will never be candidates for the coming of the light.

> *We don't need a Savior unless we suffer from sin. We never need redemption unless we're in bondage.*

I'm not promoting a gospel of suffering, but of healing. I know for certain that to the degree we choose to manipulate and avoid tough times, we also choose to miss out on the One who can give us the strength we need to face our difficulties and find our way through them. To the degree that we hide behind self-justification and rationalization, we avoid the redeeming work of the Holy Spirit.

A marriage can't be put back together until the husband wakes up and faces how selfish he has been or until the wife comes to her senses and faces her hurtful words and behavior. A young person can't resist peer pressure until he or she faces the deep need for acceptance that is driving certain choices. Counselors struggle first to get people to be honest about what is really wrong.

A Pharisee is someone who doesn't think he needs help. He is completely lost under his own hubris. "I don't need your help. I have a plan—an admirable one, a very religious one—to make it on my own, thank you!" But when we think we don't need help, to that degree—in direct proportion—we avoid the Savior.

God wants to save you where you really are, not where you wish you were, not where you think you ought to be. Jesus can help us see the reality of where we are—and He will also give us the strength we need to act on what we see. He wants to do this so that we can share in the glory of who He is. If you know that you are hedging on reality, adjusting it, hiding, attempting to rationalize the condition that you're in, let God break through for you and do for you what He did for Adam—make you see who you really are. Let

Him do for you in some measure what He did for Isaiah—help you see the future you have in Christ, no matter what your present circumstances are.

God doesn't adjust to our reality; He calls us to adjust to His. And yet, in the adjusting, we experience the gift of His deliverance. A whole new way of living opens up for us—and we discover it to be the most wonderfully real thing we've ever experienced.

ENTER, SPIRIT OF TRUTH

Lord Jesus, I'm so often afraid of reality. I'm so often hiding, blaming, avoiding—and I don't even realize it. Touch me, Jesus.

Give me strength not to turn away, but to receive Your life. With You, I can face any reality. Amen.

6

"YOU SOLD ME, HE SENT ME"

People who succeed in life—life as God originally intended—
believe that God is in control.

You're driving to church on a beautiful September Sunday morning. The fall air is brisk and still. Vine maple and oak are showing some color, and the roses are making a comeback after the heat of summer. The university kids are back in town; as you pass the park, you notice a happy group playing flag football.

"This is the day, This is the day that the Lord has made…." The verse drifts through your mind. You're looking forward to worship this morning.

Then something else drifts in. Pictures. CNN news reports. Headlines. What a week for Planet Earth! Terrorist bombings, perversion of justice, abandoned children, deadly epidemics—and in your own neighborhood, a grade-school girl is killed by a hit-and-run driver.

In a minute or two, you find yourself standing in church, family and friends around you, the organ is swelling, and you're singing with all your might, "The Whole Earth Is Full of His Glory!"

Then you hear a little voice inside your head saying, "Yeah right. Sure thing…"

Suddenly, nothing fits. Your mouth still sings along with the congregation, but your heart is asking, *Exactly which earth am I singing about? Planet Earth of this lovely September Sunday morning? Or Planet Earth of the past gruesome September week?*

Without warning, you've entered a war zone. In your spirit, you feel a savage assault on the integrity of your faith, and on the sovereignty and goodness of your God.

Every man or woman who is truly responding to God's call on his or her life will enter this conflict. In this arena, when you feel like all you hold dear is under fire, you must decide some fundamental questions about God. Is He in control? And if He's in control, why do such terrible things happen? And if He's not, what am I doing here singing His praises?

SHAPED BY A CHOICE

We all know women who were traumatized by a relative in childhood or men who've been brutalized by some crushing physical or emotional violence. We try to understand the past, and take into consideration the previous experiences of others. Terrible events in the past can help explain stupid, destructive behaviors in the present.

But most of us realize the arithmetic of circumstances never adds up to explain—or take the blame—

for how we live. Imagine a home where one parent is an alcoholic and the other is living in depression. From this difficult home comes a young man who grows up to live a destructive, wasted life. But look at his brother—he comes from that same home, but he grows up to be sensitive, kind, and responsible.

Same parents. Same problems. Same environment. Two totally different young men. Why? How? Because your environment doesn't shape you. Your responses to your environment shape you.

It's not the circumstances of your life—beautiful Septembers and tragic Septembers are both real—it's how you respond to your life that shapes you. Your responses forge your attitudes and actions and make you the person you are today—and the person you will be tomorrow.

Some of us have to accept responsibility for the circumstances we face in our lives right now. They are the harvest of seeds we have sown with our own hands. But some of us are suffering the bitter consequences of other people's misdeeds. Other people have made foolish decisions that have changed our lives forever.

If you're in the second category, I want to gently say to you that regardless of the pain that someone else may have brought into your life, no one else has the power to shape your life unless you give it to him or her. In Jesus Christ, the power to choose is available to you.

And I'm sure of this—you will never become what you want to become, let alone what God wants you to become, until you become a person who accepts responsibility for who you are and begin to respond in a godly way to life's circumstances.

> *No one else has the power to shape your life unless you give it to him or her.*

CHOOSING THE GOOD

Joseph is a powerful example of a young man who understood the responses he could choose in the circumstances of life. In Genesis 37, we see young Joseph sold into slavery by his brothers. By Genesis 41, Joseph is governor of all Egypt, second only to Pharoah in power.

God really has a sense of humor, doesn't He? Joseph's life is a roller-coaster ride—favorite son to rejected brother, chief servant to prisoner, and finally prison administrator to Pharoah's chosen ruler.

When do you think Joseph first had the thought that he was something special, that God had a destiny for his life? Was it when he escaped the pit? Lived through the betrayal in Potiphar's household? Found success even in prison? At some point, Joseph realized the awesome truth: "God got me here. God is here with me. God will accomplish good for me—even here!"

How does a man or a woman come to this way of thinking? It's one thing to believe that you are a child of God, that you'll be blessed no matter where you are. It's another thing to believe God's in control *no matter* where you are.

You might be wondering if I'm saying that God put Joseph into the pit. Did God sell him into slavery? Cast him into prison? Marry him off to a daughter of one of the priests of Egypt?

Did God do these bad things?

A "God put" way of speaking ultimately can lead us down some dead ends. Like, "God put me in my divorce." "God put me in my bankruptcy." "God put me in my moral failure."

Some Christians will look at the Joseph story and say, "God put him in prison in order to bring His plan to pass." Others will say, "No, He kept him while he was in prison."

The question of God's sovereign control versus our free will has plagued the church for centuries. Christians have literally killed other Christians in the heat of this argument. Ultimately, it is a paradox that we can't completely understand. How can God remain in charge while giving you and me the freedom of choice?

To me, the real issue is not whether God actually put Joseph there or kept him while he was there. The real issue is whether or not God surrendered His original agenda. Was He still in control? Whether He uses our choices or makes choices that we step into, the question is, "Can you believe, right now, that God is in charge?"

You're in a divorce. Your husband has just left you with three kids and no money. Is God still in control?

Your business partners made promises and now they've taken off. Their promises have gone with them, but you're left with the bills. Is God still in control?

Your body is being attacked by a debilitating illness. You didn't put it there; it's just there. Whether the doctor says that it's hereditary or whether it's the result of living on a fallen planet makes little difference to you. The fact is, you're dealing with something that could rob you of your life. Is God still in control?

I want to tell you that you will never accept responsibility for your life unless you believe that God is in charge. You cannot accept *immediate* responsibility until you believe God has accepted *ultimate* responsibility. You may come to understand your identity in Christ; you may grasp the fact that your acceptance is in Him and not based on your performance; you can even realize that life does not shape you, but that your responses to life shape you. But none of these truths will be worked out in your life to accomplish your destiny unless you settle the issue of who is ultimately in control.

People who succeed in life—life as God originally intended—believe that God is in control. In the face of terrible circumstances of their own and others' making, these people are fully convinced that He is still in control.

WHO'S IN CHARGE?

To bring this reality home we will look at the life of Joseph in one of the most difficult passages in the Bible. It's not harsh, but it's very, very hard.

After years of famine in Egypt, for which Joseph had prepared the people, he discovered that his own brothers had come to Egypt to buy grain (Genesis 42). As he stood before his unknowing brothers, he couldn't restrain himself any longer and cried out, "Have everyone go out from me." He then wept so loudly that the Egyptians in the house of Pharaoh heard him. Then, Joseph said to his bewildered brothers, "I am Joseph! Is my father still alive?"

The Bible says his brothers couldn't answer him because they were "dismayed at his presence." You bet they were dismayed! The teenage brother they had sold like livestock more than fifteen years before now stood over them as the highest ranking official in Pharoah's court. And he held in his hand the power of life and death.

Then Joseph did the unthinkable. He asked his brothers to come near him. "I am your brother, Joseph, whom you sold into Egypt. And now do not be grieved or angry with yourselves, because you sold me here; for God sent me before you to preserve life. For the famine has been in the land for these two years and there are still five years in which there will be neither plowing nor harvesting. And God sent me before you to preserve for you a remnant in the earth and to keep you alive by a great deliverance. Now therefore it was not you who sent me here, but God; and He has made me a father to Pharaoh and lord of all his household and a ruler over all the land of Egypt."

Later, in Genesis 50, when Jacob died and the brothers became afraid that Joseph would now seek retribution, he again reassured them, "Do not be afraid, for am I in the place of God? As for you, you meant evil against me, but God meant it for good, in order to bring about this present result, to preserve many people alive. So therefore, do not be afraid; I will provide for you and your little ones."

Joseph declared to his brothers, "Don't worry. God did this to me." And it's precisely at that point where we struggle—it's where I struggle. When everything hurtles out of control, or when circumstances just aren't shaping up the way we thought they would, don't we invariably ask, "'Who's in charge here?"

When the assaults come and we can't figure out why it's all happening, we get introspective: I wonder if I did something. I wonder if there is something I did that let that get to me. We turn introspective and heap guilt on ourselves. Our identity, our faith, and our sense of who is in control all come under fire.

We want to know: How did that tragedy happen? Where are the angels who are supposed to be standing round about those who fear the Lord? Did somebody take a vacation?

> *Where are the angels who are supposed to be standing round about those who fear the Lord?*

I do not believe that God pulled the trigger on your divorce. I do not believe that the Lord killed your baby or ripped the rug from underneath you financially. Most of those situations have to do with life on a fallen planet where others have failed and sometimes we've failed too.

But I do believe that in the middle of the divorce, God can bring to pass visions of life as it was supposed to be lived, without being intimidated by the choices that you or others have made. He can and He will—if you'll return to a position of trust and faith in Him. He only needs for you to stay in that place of grace where you really do depend upon Him. Where you trust Him. Where you love Him with the kind of devotion that says, "I'm not moving. All of this has changed, but I'm not moving."

A QUESTION OF INTENTION

All of us have our dreams that seem to have evaporated. We carry around our little suitcase of things gone wrong. If we were very honest, some of us would say, "I'm not where I want to be in terms of life's situations." Paul certainly understood that feeling, yet he confidently declared, "Yes, but here's what we know. When God is in them, all things work together."

Read Paul's familiar and wonderful affirmation again; you'll find it in Romans 8:28. Thousands of years after Joseph's declaration, Paul says that *everything* in life can be infused with divine energy to produce something good for us—if we abide in the love and calling of the Lord.

"I've signed on to His agenda," Paul is saying. "I belong to Him. I want my life to be about where He's going because I love Him and know that His calling is for certain, and because everything He is allowing has the power to be called something good."

Now listen to Joseph's words to his brothers again: "Don't be sorry. What you intended for evil, God meant for good. I know you sold me. *But even though you sold me, He sent me.*"

Do you hear that language? "You sold me. He sent me." In the middle of the circumstances that plague your life and are the results of choices you or others have made—God is still in control.

You may be facing some tough circumstances. In the middle of pain, it's hard to say that God is still in control. Sometimes we say it reluctantly or dejectedly: "Well, God's still in control." We mean that God's up there in control all right, but in some far-off place— and without a lot of heart for our particular problem.

Joseph's testimony invites us to say it genuinely— and experience great peace: "God, You're in control! Right here and right now! Every bad thing that's ever happened, somehow through Your power can be released for good, if I'll stay in the place where I believe in You and Your sovereignty and who You are."

When we don't think God is in charge, then we start giving away responsibility by blaming others. We find it difficult to forgive. But Joseph said, "You're forgiven. I'm not going to be God. God's in charge, so I don't need to be. I forgive you."

God hasn't given up on you, no matter what your circumstances. What He said He will do for you, He's still going to do. It may not happen in the way you thought, but it's going to happen. It will work for good.

Your response in light of this truth makes all the

difference: Conduct yourself in such a way that He can fulfill His promise to you. Get into position—in attitude and in action! Stand on the fact that God can turn trials and the evil deeds of others into good in your life. Be the kind of person through whom God can accomplish His agenda because you believe.

YOU ARE LORD OF ALL

Lord Jesus, come to me, as You did to Joseph, with gentle reminders of Your presence, with words of hope for my future.

I believe You will be true to Your Word, no matter what obstacles I face in my life. Give me strength and peace as I wait for Your salvation. Amen.

PART THREE

A Promise of Power

7
LIFE IN THE KING'S DOMAIN

We are empowered to live as children of the King—not by
rules and procedures—but by the Holy Spirit within us.

I f you were asked to choose one phrase that best
describes the message of Jesus while He was on earth,
what would it be? You might say, "Oh, it has to be love."
Or, "His main message was forgiveness." You might
choose mercy—going the second mile with people. Any
of these themes would be accurate to a point.

Yet one phrase captures the focus of Jesus' earthly
ministry more than any other: *the kingdom of God.*
That emphasis, woven through the Gospels from
beginning to end, is the definitive phrase of Jesus'
earthly ministry. For three years, He preached about
and lived out the kingdom of God. Even after His hor-
rendous experience on the cross and His triumphant
resurrection, He was still talking about the kingdom.

His call to you today—in the present tense, in
continuous experience, right now!—is to live in His
kingdom.

The term *kingdom* originated in fifteenth century
Britain from two words: "king's domain." Over the
years, the two words became one: "king-dom." Yet
the word retains the original meaning: the sphere of

influence, or domain, of a king. In the king's domain, the king is both the law and the power. Everything gets done the way the king likes it.

Believers today know that Jesus Christ was and is King. But many also assume that when He left the earth, Jesus took the kingdom with Him, and that when He returns, He'll bring it back with Him. But Jesus says, "If I cast out demons by the finger of God, then the kingdom of God has come upon you" (Luke 11:20). He means that whenever some kind of deliverance from darkness or evil takes place; whenever someone is released from bondage in the psyche or the soul, whether it's a false mind-set or something in the character—the kingdom of God is manifested.

Jesus lays it out for us: "Seek first His kingdom and His righteousness; and all these things shall be added to you" (Matthew 6:33). In the Greek, this command carried with it the sense of "priorities." If you will prioritize your life around the King's domain, then everything else can fall into place. His admonition is reason enough to try to understand Christ's emphasis on the kingdom of God—what the kingdom of God is, and what it is not.

MORE THAN MEAT AND DRINK

In Romans 14, Paul says, "The kingdom of God is not eating and drinking..." But he's not talking about abstaining from anything at the table. Rather, Paul is addressing two groups of people.

The first group is comprised of people whose view of God is very strained. They believe that God has a lot of difficulty dealing with human imperfections, and so they walk very nervously before Him. Their conception of God is full of "Don't drink this and don't eat that because, if you do, God will get mad at you." Paul describes these men and women as being weak in conscience. Don't mistake an overactive conscience for strong faith, Paul seems to be saying; their faith in God's power to redeem is actually underdeveloped.

The second group views God as someone who understands human imperfections and deficiencies. They believe that His concern for us goes much deeper than what we eat or what we drink. Paul says these people have a strong conscience.

It's to those with the stronger conscience, that Paul says, "Listen, you have a healthy view of God. You are mature in your faith and strong in conscience. Therefore, the responsibility to conduct yourself in such a way that you don't cause pain to those who are weaker in their faith rests on you. The greater responsibility is yours because you have the larger picture. So don't eat things that will cause them to be at pain in their conscience, or drink things that will cause them to stumble."

But as soon as Paul finishes addressing those of stronger conscience, his next statement is the one that we just read, "The Kingdom of God is not meat and drink." Amazing isn't it? After he goes on at some length about how different persons view eating and drinking, he then says that, the truth is, the Kingdom of God isn't about meat and drink anyway!

Paul wants the Christians of Rome to understand an important principle: "The kingdom of God is *not* rules and regulations." Even if we think we understand this truth, we can quickly become confused. We slip into thinking that if we live a certain way, we can experience the power of God's kingdom. But it doesn't matter how holy and how pure we try to be. Even if we did everything letter-perfect, our perfection wouldn't ensure that we would experience the kingdom of God.

You're in the kingdom for only one reason—because of your allegiance to the King. Once you are in His kingdom, you discover how to live. But the blueprint won't be given to you on paper. It will be put in your heart by the Holy Spirit. We live by the Spirit, not by a set of rules and regulations. Kingdom life is not codified behavior or harsh legalism. It's not God standing above us with a big rock saying, "You do that, and I'm going to drop this thing right on top of your head."

Not at all. When we are released from the kingdom of darkness and ushered into the kingdom of Jesus, we experience a new dimension of freedom. Now we are accepted in the Beloved. We are saved by grace and empowered to live as a child of the King—not by policies and procedures—but by the power of the Holy Spirit.

> *You're in the kingdom for only one reason—because of your allegiance to the King.*

THE ANOINTING THAT ABIDES

John describes life in the King's domain as the anointing that abides. The anointing means you don't need somebody to tell you what is wrong or right—you have been touched by the Holy One. In the King's domain, we have the promise of an inner guidance system of His Spirit in continual communion with our spirit.

I've found that when I experience this working of the Spirit in my life, my decisions have substance. I may not always be able to list for you the exact reasons why I can or can't do something, but the decisions are based on sound thinking. I experience a strong, clear direction in me that either says, "No, don't" or "Yes, let's do that." What is that sense? It is the unction from the Holy One, the anointing that abides.

The truth of the presence and power of the kingdom of God has been making people nervous since the time of Jesus. In Luke 17, we read of Pharisees coming to Jesus, demanding to know when the kingdom of God will arrive. Like a lot of good Christians today, those Pharisees believed in the afterlife, in a returning Savior, in living above reproach, and in striving to please God. But everything was external for them. Their motto might as well have been, "Dress right; talk right; eat right; wash right—and you'll be all right."

They confronted Jesus. "You've been teaching for two and a half years about this kingdom," they said. "So when is the kingdom of God going to come?"

Jesus replied, "The kingdom of God does not come with your careful observation, nor will people say, 'Here it is' or 'There it is,' because the kingdom of God is within you."

You see, the Pharisees based everything on "careful observation." But Jesus wanted them to see that His kingdom was going to happen in another way. It wouldn't arrive by any external means—religious performance, a human ruler, or liberating army.

Then Jesus delivered the punch line. "In fact," He said, "the kingdom of God is here and now—it is within you." The Pharisees were shocked. They had merely wanted to know when it was coming so they could jump on the bandwagon. And here was Jesus telling them, "The kingdom of God is here already. I'm here, standing in the midst of you. And My kingdom is immediately available!"

How easily we, too, miss the fact that He is in our midst!

Whenever you welcome the person of Jesus Christ into your life as King, whenever you invite Him to come with all of His authority into a particular situation or concern—in that very moment, the King's domain is immediately available to you.

Don't be trapped into thinking that the kingdom is an "exterior phenomenon." The kingdom of God is within.

The apostle Paul understood this. He saw that the Corinthians were proud about their religious ideas and spiritual philosophies. To them he said, "The kingdom of God is not in word but in power" (1 Corinthians 4:20).

Paul wanted the Corinthian believers to see that knowledge and theories about the kingdom don't matter. The bottom line is this:

The kingdom of God isn't theory—it's experience.

The kingdom of God isn't formula—it's force.

The kingdom of God isn't principle—it's power.

The kingdom of God isn't talked—it's walked.

And who is a candidate for this power? Only the

apostle Paul or those like him? No! We don't have to wait to become holy or spiritual. Jesus taught about the kingdom to poor widows, fishermen, tax collectors, dusty country folk. Paul wrote about the kingdom to distracted, overscheduled, well-scrubbed city folk. Do you see it? Wherever Jesus is King, the kingdom of God is available now. Available to people like you and me.

THE JOY OF THE KING

But let's go deeper. We learn in Romans 14:17 the qualities that make up the kingdom of God: "righteousness and peace and joy in the Holy Spirit."

We can easily misinterpret the verse to mean: "If I can just be righteous I can experience the kingdom, I can experience peace, I can just be happy." Instead reverse it! Experience the kingdom—and you'll be right. Experience the kingdom—and you'll have peace. Experience the kingdom—and you'll have the joy of the Holy Spirit. Righteousness, peace, and joy are not the prerequisites for kingdom life, but its natural outcomes.

Let the Holy Spirit reveal to you the truth of what it means to be a kingdom person. In a difficult situation, believe that Jesus Christ is King. Surrender to His authority. He'll make you righteous. He'll grant you peace. He'll give you the joy of the Holy Spirit.

A dear friend was experiencing the joy of the Holy

Spirit even though he had recently lost his little boy. One day he said to me, "I still have tough times when I go in the woods because we used to go to the woods a lot together. But there's a joy in me that I can't explain." How could this man have any joy in the midst of such pain?

Let me try to explain by using a word picture. Imagine with me that life is a motion picture. Imagine the film playing past the light of the projection camera one frame at a time. Frame. Frame. Frame...

Most of us see our lives like that. We focus on one frame at a time: Frame. Frame. Frame... That's all we see.

But joy in the Spirit comes because the Holy Spirit sees the whole film at once. God can see the whole story from beginning to end, and what He sees in the whole film makes Him very happy. He knows things we don't know. Because He has the big picture, His joy is complete and bubbles up inside us.

You won't always know specifically why you're happy. In fact, there may be nothing in your present circumstances to be happy about. Yet the Holy Spirit sees something that makes Him happy—and He wants to share that with you and through you.

The joy of the Holy Spirit is available to you as you surrender to the King. Believe that He's in your midst. In frustrating situations or confusing emotions, welcome the King. Receive Him. That's when you will experience the kingdom. Righteousness, peace, and joy in the Holy Spirit are the proof.

> *God can see the whole story from beginning to end,*
> *and what He sees in the whole film*
> *makes Him very happy.*

And the kingdom of God is not a spiritualized compartment in our lives. Sometimes we think when we're in church we're closer to the kingdom. Afterward we go home to a difficult marriage or to a terrible job or to challenging kids. But the "sphere of influence" of the King's domain covers *everything*. Whatever we surrender to Jesus as King becomes His kingdom— marriage, parenting, business, our own heart and mind.

Remember that Jesus taught us to pray, "Thy kingdom come, thy will be done." And He wasn't talking about a pie-in-the-sky, somewhere-down-the-line kingdom.

Follow after Jesus. Embrace His Lordship daily. Live today as a child of the King. His kingdom is immediately available to you if Jesus is immediately King.

JESUS, BE KING

Lord Jesus, come and be King of my life. By Your power, bind and release, heal and set free. By Your Spirit, anoint me to fully experience Your kingdom. Every corner and closet of my life is Your domain. I seek You and Your kingdom first. Amen.

8
WHEN THE MOMENT COMES

Knowing your true identity is the secret
to successfully resisting temptation.

Temptation.

It's not a subject we like to talk about. Yet if you love God and desire to follow Jesus, you'll one day face the crisis of temptation—and often many daily testings along the way. With each temptation comes an opportunity to compromise in some area of your life, to betray some truth. And the truth is usually about who you are.

Some men and women seem to have such a clear grasp of God's goodness and His perspective on their lives that at the moment of temptation, they find their way through. For us, the obvious questions are, "Why do some stand firm through temptation—and others fall headlong? What makes the difference?"

An episode out of the life of Joseph provides a surprising answer and a powerful insight. You'll recall that Joseph had proved himself as the accomplished administrator of the household of Potiphar, the captain of Pharaoh's guard (Genesis 39). Potiphar noticed that everything Joseph touched prospered, "so he left everything he owned in Joseph's care; and with him there, did not concern himself with anything except the food which he ate" (Genesis 39:6).

The temptation came in the form of Potiphar's wife. And it came at a time when Joseph commanded the kind of authority that would have allowed him to compromise and still protect himself. With his power and responsibilities, it would have been easy for him to enjoy the pleasures of sin, then make arrangements to cover up his deed.

THE REFUGE OF IDENTITY

One day when she made her advances, encouraging him to commit sexual sin, Joseph responded, "I'm not going to lie with you. I know who I am. I know what's right. I know what's wrong. I know who God is. This would be transgression against Him, against what He has told me I am, against the dream He gave me. I know who I am because I know who He is, and I know my destiny is with Him. I can't act any other way. I can't live any other way. To do so would compromise who I am." In effect, Joseph was saying that even though he now lived as a slave, he hadn't forgotten who he was.

But doing the right thing only got Joseph thrown in prison! Yet even there, the Lord was with Joseph, and soon he was running the prison for the chief guard. It didn't matter where circumstances took Joseph—pit, prison, or palace—God kept showing up!

Think this through with me: Did God bless Joseph because of his conduct and performance? Or did the blessing of God rest upon Joseph because of who he was, no matter where he was?

Joseph knew the answer. He knew he was chosen of God. He knew his identity was secure. It was the one thing he could not surrender.

It's exactly what we see in Joseph's answer to Potiphar's wife. He knew who he was: "How then can I do this great evil, and sin against God?" (Genesis 39:9).

When a temptation begins to weaken our resolve, our tendency is to disqualify ourselves. "Maybe I'm not the person I thought I was," we say. Or, "If I were a real Christian, I wouldn't be so strongly tempted about this." Or, "God is probably disgusted with me by now anyway." Do you see how we begin to call our very identity into question? Compromise begins to seem reasonable. We become confused about the most important things.

Not Joseph.

> Compromise begins to seem reasonable. We become confused about the most important things.

He knew who he was. And he had not changed: "I am a favored son. I am not going to compromise myself." Catch this: "I've had to let go of my dream, but I'm not letting go of the One who gave me the dream."

When we're enticed to reach for what isn't ours, or relinquish our God-given dreams because of our own failures, we must remember who, and whose, we are. Blessing rests upon a man or woman whom God has chosen, on the one who has responded to Jesus Christ. We are *in* Him. We enjoy a privileged position of grace because God chose us before the foundation of the world. He's appointed each of us to be a person of destiny.

People who understand their positions can live like Joseph. Because they know who they are, they can make it through the webs of deception, through pits of rejection, through slavery, through imprisonment, without acting like either a slave or a prisoner.

FALLING INTO GRACE

But what about the ones who surrender in that moment of temptation? What about those who don't make it?

People who don't make it, who give up their hope in the God who is the giver of dreams, fall into the trap of believing that practice produces favor, that performance brings about blessing. They've forgotten that the base, the foundation of our day-to-day relationship with God through Jesus Christ is always grace.

I want you to know that I've been faithful to my

wife. I've never committed adultery. Still I've slept with Potiphar's wife. Watch carefully: Scripture is literal, but it is also representative. Potiphar's wife was a real person, and her story is a literal, physical lesson for us. But Scripture is representative as well, and here Potiphar's wife represents all kinds of enticements.

You can commit adultery without ever having a sexual experience. That's why the scripture says, "You adulteresses, do you not know that friendship with the world is hostility toward God?" (James 4:4). You can sleep with the world.

I've got to admit that I've done that. I've made serious errors in my Christian life, and every time I've fallen, it's always been because I've taken my eyes off of who I am in Christ Jesus. Identity is the secret to successfully resisting temptation.

Those who do not resist the opportunities for compromise and temptation are men and women who have become shortsighted or blinded and have forgotten who they are. They have forgotten that they were purged from their sins.

Jesus Himself, immediately after His baptism and glorious approval by the Father, is taken into the wilderness. The first thing He hears in His encounter with Satan relates to the subject of identity.

As He is being baptized, what does He hear? "You are My Son."

What does He hear the devil say? *"If* you are the Son of God..."

This juxtaposition gives us tremendous insight. *Every time sin comes to seduce, it's always an attack on our identity.*

Inevitably you will encounter people or circumstances that will tempt you to think you're still under the power of darkness. It's then that you must decide whom you will believe. Will you allow your circumstances to define your position, or will you let God's truth define your position? People who forget who they are go ahead and lie with Potiphar's wife. At the time, it makes all the sense in the world.

> *Identity is the secret*
> *to successfully resisting temptation.*

The way to resist, the way to win the battle is to stand on who you are in Christ. "No, I'm not going to compromise who I am. I'm not going to live another way. It doesn't matter if they do this to me, or do that to me—I can't compromise who I am. I won't."

This understanding is vital to experiencing life as God intended it. Paul spends a great deal of time in Ephesians emphasizing our position in Christ: "We have been seated in heavenly places with Christ. We have been raised with Christ to heavenly places. We have a new place. We have a new position. In Christ, we have changed locations."

When Paul writes to the Colossians, he says, "You've been moved to a new place by an act of God's power. You're rescued out of the power of darkness and put into a new position. This new position is in the kingdom—under the rule of Jesus Christ."

Our resolve to embrace our position in Christ, however imperfectly we may carry it out, brings with it the power not only to resist the enemy but to live in a way that makes room for the blessings of God. God will show up just as He did for Joseph, whether we are in prison or the palace, whether we're being rejected or honored, and whether we think our dream is dead or alive.

MY IDENTITY IN YOU SETS ME FREE

Lord Jesus, I am so grateful that I belong to You. I trust in Your power, not my own. Show me more and more of who I am in You. By Your Spirit, teach me, Lord Jesus. Amen.

9
THE RADICAL PARTNERSHIP

*Everything you are has to be invested in order to receive
the miraculous return of everything He is.*

In the life of the kingdom, we come to moments when the torch is passed from one person to another, from one generation to the next. A man or woman of God senses in his or her heart that God is assigning a new task—and giving the necessary power of His life to accomplish that task.

I am constrained by the Holy Spirit to offer you a possibility: This may be your moment. Now may be the time when you should stir the gift He has deposited within you and prepare yourself for the moment when the torch will be passed…to you.

In one of Paul's final conversations with Timothy, we see such a moment played out for this young man (2 Timothy 1). Paul says to the one he has mentored and cared for, "Listen, stop being afraid. I was there. I laid hands on you. I know what was put into you. You've got something from your grandmother. You've got something from your mother. You've got something from me. You've got something from Almighty God. Now stir up the gift and use it!"

The passing of the torch. For those of you chosen and ordained by God for the work of His kingdom, a similar moment will come. How will we understand and anticipate such a personal miracle?

WITH GOD IN DEEP WATER

Let's look at a scene from the life of Christ for insight on how to "stir up the gift and use it" in our own personal lives. In Luke 5, we read that as Jesus was teaching by the Sea of Galilee, the crowd "listening to the word of God" was so great that it literally pressed against Him—possibly threatening to push Him into the lake.

At the water's edge were two fishing boats, one of which belonged to Simon Peter. Jesus' solution was to borrow the boat, and He asked Peter to push out a little ways into the water. Then Jesus sat down in the boat and spoke to the crowds from there.

While Jesus taught, I imagine Peter at the back of the boat preoccupied with washing nets or tending to other chores left over from a night's work—a night that had been all work and no fish.

When Jesus finished teaching, He turned to Peter and issued a remarkable invitation, "Let's go out to the deep water. I want you to let down your nets for a catch."

Now Peter's nets might have been ready, but his

attitude wasn't. "Master, we have toiled all night, and we haven't caught anything." (Can you see the blank look on Peter's face?) Then he relented: "But if you want, we will do it. At Your word, I'll let down the net." And that's exactly what Jesus had in mind. So Peter, followed by the second boat, rowed out into the lake to fish.

Luke records that when Peter pulled the nets back in, he had caught so many fish the nets began to break. Excited, Peter yelled to the others within range to come and help haul in the nets. But that wasn't the end of Peter's surprise—unbelievably, so many fish now filled the boat that they began to sink.

Peter was stunned by the size of the catch. He had fished all his life—and he knew this couldn't be happening. But it was. Something had happened that he couldn't explain. Or maybe he could. "This ain't fishing," you can hear him gasping. "This is a miracle!"

Peter dropped to his knees right in the middle of all those fish and cried out to Jesus, "Get away from me, Lord. I'm a sinful man!"

This may seem like a strange reaction, but Jesus' response was immediate. "Don't be afraid," he said to this anxious fisherman. "From now on you are going to catch people. Not fish. People."

Now let's stop the action for a minute and work back through the story to see what the Lord will show us as we consider our assignment and destiny and the admonition to "stir up the gift within us."

PRESSING CLOSER

Notice the Scriptures say that the people pressed about Jesus to hear the "word of God." Why was there such tremendous interest? Because people knew that when they came to Jesus they would hear what God had to say. You see, God wants you to hear the word of the Lord, not simply read and learn Bible text. He wants you to hear directly from Jesus. He wants you to hear His word for your life—and the hunger for hearing God is what still brings crowds today. To stir up your gift and prepare for your assignment, you must press close to Jesus to hear what God will say to you personally. Only then will you have something of power and meaning to say to others.

> *God wants to you to hear the word of the Lord, not simply read and learn Bible text. He wants you to hear directly from Jesus.*

Scripture says, "He sat down and taught the multitudes from the boat." I find great beauty in this phrase. If you're going to be ready to take the torch and run, you must settle the issue of style versus substance or it will distract you in the race. In our culture we're usually all hung up on one or the other. In this picture of Jesus teaching from the boat, we have the lovely blending of both. How amazing to think the God of the Universe taught while "sitting down in a boat"!

You are free to express the message that God has deposited within you in a way that fits your circumstances and is uniquely you. As you become confident about who you are, you'll find that *how* you express the life of Jesus will manifest itself differently in you than in any other Christian brother or sister. Personal expression flows naturally when you know what God wants to say. But if you are not hearing from the Lord or speaking His message, no amount of personal style or polish will help you touch the life of another with the life of God.

Because Jesus is invisible, it is His Word that makes His presence known. When you take the time to hear from God personally, people near you will experience the influence of God on your life. They will know that it is a miracle of the Spirit, and that something of His life is flowing out of you. The disciples on the road to Emmaus described the experience this way: "When we heard Him, our hearts burned."

A LIFE ON LOAN

I want us to notice the wonderful way that the Lord mentors, how He pulls men and women into partnership with Himself. When it comes time for Jesus to move you into partnership, He often asks to use something that belongs to you. To partner in the miraculous ministry of Jesus will cost you something—usually something you hold dear.

Jesus comes in His lovely way to reveal our destiny. But inevitably our assignment has something to do with possession. It is always tied to something that you have personal control over—your time, your money, your home. It is almost astonishing how accurately He zeroes in on *that one thing*.

These are the delightful ways that Jesus invites us into partnership. We'd rather develop tidy little courses and write books about the doctrine of a disciple, the character of a disciple, or the availability of a disciple. But discipleship by Jesus requires a complete exchange. Everything you are has to be invested in order to receive the return of everything He is.

You already may have begun to experience His supernatural provision in many areas of your life. You may be learning certain skills, moving with a new sense of power and authority in your spiritual and personal life. You're excited about the fruitfulness that is beginning to happen. But make no mistake about it, somewhere along the line, in order for Him to do all these wonderful things He wants to do through you, He will walk into your life and say to you as He did to Peter, the fisherman, "Excuse me! Could I use your boat?"

HOW MIRACLES HAPPEN

As we mature in partnering, eventually we will arrive at the wonderful opportunity to go further. Jesus will say to us, "OK, launch out into the deep. Let down your net for a catch."

Those around you might say that if you're catching some fish and the boat isn't sinking, God is with you and you should hold on to what you've got. But I challenge you to think differently. When God is an active partner in a venture, you can't keep up with the returns. You're always trying to catch up. Think about it: When we have a task all figured out, then that's all it will ever be—something we can figure out on our own.

Jesus says, "Launch out into the deep. Get ready for the catch of your life!" Oh, how we need to hear Jesus say that in our own personal lives. How we need the miraculous! The miraculous power that causes nets to break and boats to sink. When you begin to partner with Jesus, miracles will take place.

If we look at what this story teaches about miracles, we could say that the miraculous always begins with something you can do. Jesus only asked Peter to "launch out." He didn't ask him to produce the catch! But often the miraculous also begins with something you don't want to do. It requires time, energy, or resources that you'd rather not expend. It's all about fishing where you've already fished—just because He asks you to.

> *The miraculous always begins with something you can do.*

How we need the miraculous! And how we resist it out of fear! We're so afraid it won't or *can't* happen. Watch for those impressions in your inner being, the fleeting thought that says, "I don't know what will come of it, but I think we ought to do something here." At those moments, for heaven's sake, stop and do something! Give the Lord an opportunity to break something loose. Do the possible. Don't do something crazy, just the simple, obedient thing. Listen to His voice, and follow.

As you do the possible, God is released to do the impossible—to do the part that only He can do. Our task is to make room for Him. Live with the constant awareness of how much we need the miraculous.

THE CATCH

Now we come to the most touching moment of this wonderful story of Peter.

Prior to this time—probably many days or weeks earlier—Peter had heard the call of Jesus to "Come, follow Me." The Scriptures say that Peter and those with him left everything to follow Jesus. But now some time has passed, and they have gone back to fishing. *Ironically,* Jesus just happens to be there on the shore with the crowds the morning that Peter returns from fishing all night.

Isn't it interesting that it would be Peter's boat that Jesus asks for? "Say, Peter, can I use your boat?"

Out on the water, in the deep waters of the Sea of Galilee, the net is filled. And then the fish begin to break the net and threaten to sink the boat. Peter is as much horrified and ashamed as he is overwhelmed by what is taking place. And then comes his heartfelt cry, "Stand away from me, I am full of sin. Get away from me, because I know this is a miracle, and I don't deserve this."

I hear myself saying it all the time: *Lord, I'm full of sin. I'm not worthy of what is happening to me. I don't belong in this crowd—I know the stuff that's in me, and I'm figuring out what's in You—and we shouldn't be anywhere near each other! Get away from me.*

So often, we cry out with thoughts of unworthiness or we compare ourselves with others. We cry, "I'll never be like him. I'll never be like her. I'm not worthy of net-breaking, boat-sinking miracles."

And in that moment, Jesus responds to Peter and to all of us: "Don't be afraid." He understands why we would feel frightened, overwhelmed, and unworthy, but He immediately says, "Stop it!"

You may sense that God is preparing you for a significant assignment. A big catch. But you don't need to be afraid.

Every single one of us could say to Jesus, "Stand away. I'm not worthy!" But hear what Jesus wants to say to you: "Stop being afraid. I've got fish for you to catch that you can't even imagine. I've got a destiny that can only happen through miracles! Let Me break your nets!—the limits of your understanding and expectation. If your dream isn't bigger than your net, then it's not Me in your boat!"

Jesus desires to bring new skill levels into your life for the express purpose of fulfilling the assignment He has given you. Press close to Jesus to hear what God is saying to *you!* Just you. Allow His message to be expressed clearly through your life in a way that honors the unique creation He made you to be.

And expect Jesus to ask to use your boat. In His kind of radical partnership, He always will.

LORD, ALL I HAVE IS YOURS

Lord Jesus, by Your grace, accomplish new giftings and new fruitfulness in me. Take what You need from my life, Lord. Use what is precious to me. Use my boat!

Help me to be open to Your wonderful miracles. Lord Jesus, the torch is passing, and I desire to partner with You in Your great plan. Amen.

PART FOUR

The Promise of Destiny

10

DREAMING GOD'S WAY

Too often we have enough faith to believe in God's blessings,
but not enough faith to believe in His methods and timing.

On vivid display within the first few pages of the Bible is a human tendency to hear a word from God, and then try—my way—to make it come to pass.

God tells Cain and Abel how to receive His blessing. Cain's response—"I'm going to do it my way!"

God blesses mankind with skills and abilities that bring them wealth and prosperity. The people decide to build the Tower of Babel so they can reach God and make a name for themselves. "We're going to do it our way!"

Abraham hears God's promise that he'll have a son with his wife, Sarah, but he can't wait, so he fathers Ishmael with his wife's maid. Generations of conflict and bloodshed are the result. "I'm going to do it my way!"

Did you ever wonder why we think we somehow have to help God make His purposes come to pass? Why do we try to justify our actions and manipulations? The answer is simple: *We have enough faith to believe in God's blessings but not enough to believe in His methods and timing.* We are unable to claim and live out the dream God's way.

In the story of Isaac and Rebekah and their two sons, Jacob and Esau, we encountered another family who tried to make God's promise happen their way. They were caught in manipulation and deception as a result. It's a particularly tragic story in light of how much God had already blessed the family. A father and his two sons manipulated God's plan, while the mother put on the finishing touches of deceit.

In ancient times, when the family wealth was distributed the firstborn received as his "birthright" twice as much as everyone else. After God told Abraham that great blessing would come to the earth through his family line, the idea of the birthright carried even more significance in his family.

You can imagine how baffling it would have been for Isaac and Rebekah to learn before the birth of their twins that the "older will serve the younger." Even though the working out of the prophecy was God's problem, several key players in this family story took matters into their own hands and created painful consequences for everyone.

A MOMENT OF WEAKNESS

One day, when the boys had grown to young men, Esau returned from the field after a long day of hunting. He was famished and decided to bargain with Jacob for a bowl of hot stew. Jacob seized the opportunity to persuade Esau to sell his birthright—the right of the firstborn—in exchange for stew. How could Esau, in a moment of hunger and weariness, give away so much for so little? After his hunger was satisfied, Esau wondered the same thing. The Scriptures tell us that soon he wept bitterly over his mistake.

On closer look, Esau's story begins to sound familiar. He had an intense need, and he wanted immediate relief. The spiritual dimension—being part of God's big plan—didn't make much sense in that condition. He figured, "If I die of hunger, being 'firstborn' isn't going to make much of a difference." He wasn't thinking *forever*. He was only thinking *now*. Sound familiar?

Most of us, I think, if we're honest at all, will have to admit that we make foolish, shortsighted decisions when we're tired. The end of the day, when you're drained and exhausted, is a poor time to consider whether you're going to stay married to that man you call your husband or the woman who is your wife.

When we're worn out, we tend to make arrangements aimed at protecting ourselves or in some other way bringing immediate relief. We switch focus from the important problem to the urgent problem. Some of us have turned our backs on walking with the Lord Jesus simply because we've gotten tired of it. Some of you have had an assignment for a certain season that has been very exacting, and you've given up. You've concluded, "I can't go on. I am too weary."

At some point, each of us has surrendered his birthright and, in some sense, lost some measure of destiny for a bowl of soup. Esau's life serves as a powerful reminder: *Physical or emotional weariness can cause us to lose track of God's faithfulness*—and position us for deception.

> We switch focus from the important problem
> to the urgent problem.

DESPERATE MOVES

The transaction between Esau and Jacob set the stage for the next part of this Genesis soap opera. Many years later, Isaac, the father, was old and in failing health. He decided it was time to bestow his blessing on his firstborn. In spite of the prophecy regarding the "older serving the younger," or the fact that Esau long ago gave away his birthright, Isaac called for Esau, his firstborn, to give him a blessing.

It came to pass, when Isaac was old…that he called Esau his older son and said to him, "My son…. Behold now, I am old. I do not know the day of my death. Now therefore, please take your weapons, your quiver and your bow,

and go out to the field and hunt game for me.
And make me savory food, such as I love, and
bring it to me that I may eat, that my soul may
bless you before I die." (Genesis 27:1–4, NKJV)

Enter Rebekah. Neither the father nor the elder
son realized that Mom was standing nearby, overhear-
ing the conversation. As soon as Esau was out of sight,
Rebekah went to Jacob, her favorite son, and convinced him to play the part of Esau in order to fool
Isaac into bestowing the blessing on him instead of his
elder son. He could substitute a goat for wild game.

But Jacob was skeptical. He told his mother the
plan would never work because Isaac would reach out
and touch his arm and know by the feel of his arm that
he wasn't Esau. In a revealing moment, Jacob said,
"Mother, I'll seem to be a deceiver to him and instead
of getting a blessing, I'll get a curse."

Undaunted, Rebekah assured him that she would
take the curse upon herself if Isaac uncovered the plan,
and she pressured Jacob. Jacob decided to obey, and
Rebekah prepared her husband's favorite food, dressed
Jacob to appear to be Esau, and sent him in to his
father.

Rebekah perhaps best illustrates how easily we can
fool ourselves into thinking we must help God along
in accomplishing His plan, in fulfilling His promise to

us. She knew the promise of God yet gave way to fear that the promise might not come to pass. This fear, this unbelief, can lead to terrible deception that will ensnare us and eventually those around us.

I'm sure you can relate to this dilemma in some area of your life. Has God said He's going to restore your marriage—and it's not happening? Do you believe God has promised to prosper your business— and things have never been worse? Do you believe that the Lord is going to heal you—but your symptoms sure don't show it yet? Do you love another person and feel convinced he or she is God's best for you—but the other person isn't hearing the same word from the Lord?

What do we do now? Our decision in these times may seem to turn on how smart we are or how much initiative we can bring to the situation. But it doesn't. Our decision comes down to how much we trust God.

Rebekah took matters into her own hands and persuaded her son to join her in lying to her husband. It's a repulsive thought to most of us, and yet when our fears and unbelief get the best of us, we can be tempted to operate in the same manner. Esau stumbled over hunger mixed with doubt. Rebekah went astray by doubt joined with opportunity. The opportunity was to use her greatest personal strengths—initiative and courage—to "help God out."

Rebekah's story gives us another important principle: *Unbelief drives us to manipulation.*

A SETUP FOR DECEPTION

Jacob stood in the presence of his father. At first, Jacob had a little trouble convincing Isaac that he was Esau—after all, he returned too quickly with hunted game. But Jacob thought fast. "The Lord your God brought the game to me," he told his father.

I don't know about you, but this really bothers me. It's one thing to lie to your parent or to steal from your brother, but now Jacob has resorted to claiming the Lord as an "ally!"

After his scrumptious meal, Isaac called Jacob to come close to him so that he could bestow the blessing.

"Come near now and kiss me, my son." And he came near and kissed him; and he [Isaac] smelled the smell of his clothing, and blessed him and said: "Surely, the smell of my son is like the smell of a field which the LORD has blessed. Therefore may God give you of the dew of heaven, of the fatness of the earth, and plenty of grain and wine. Let peoples serve you, and nations bow down to you. Be master over your brethren, and let your mother's sons bow down to you. Cursed be everyone who

curses you, blessed be those who bless you!"
(Genesis 27:26–29, NKJV)

No sooner did Isaac finish blessing Jacob than Esau
returned from the field. He was heartbroken as Isaac
told him that he had just made his brother, Jacob, master over him. It was a broken son who addressed his
father: "And Esau said to his father, 'Have you only one
blessing, my father? Bless me; me also, O my father!'
And Esau lifted up his voice and wept."

But all Isaac had left was a gloomy prophecy about
Esau staying alive by the sword and serving his
younger brother. The biblical record closes the scene
with a disheartening statement: "Esau hated Jacob."

It's almost easy to feel sorry for Isaac. After all, the
old man only wanted one last good meal before he
died. And in the process, he was betrayed by his son
and his wife. But we should remember that Isaac knew
the prophecy that the older of his sons would serve the
younger.

Why did this man of God ignore God's prophecy
and choose to bless the older son? For the same reason
we often let go of the promises of God or decide on
our own timing in a situation. Like Esau before him,
Isaac was set up to be deceived by a simple human
impulse—his appetite.

Hasn't it happened to you? I've had it happen.

Hungry for this. Hungry for that. Sex or material wealth or prestige—on any front, when I desire something outside of the Lord's way, then I set myself up to be taken advantage of.

Picture Isaac, blind and groping, smelling the "venison," hearing the voice. It's so pathetic. It shouldn't be too difficult for us to take Isaac out of the picture and put ourselves in his place. Does it look familiar? When we let our desires motivate our decisions, we go blind. Our feelings and senses get warped. We become easily confused.

Isaac becomes for us a third reminder of what makes us vulnerable to the temptation of not trusting God: When desire rules, the stage is set for my deception.

> *When we let our desires motivate our decisions, we go blind. Our feelings and senses get warped.*

CHEATING FOR THE BLESSING

In this painfully human drama, Jacob came the closest to some attempt at decency. At least he protested. Remember when he said, "No, Mama, we can't do this"? He must have been shocked at the measure of unbelief in his mother and the kind of deception she asked him to take part in.

Unfortunately after the initial protest, he played

the part all too well. Hear the lie: "I am Esau." See the duplicity of it all. Hear him use the arrogance of spiritual words and spiritual language so smoothly. It was a pathetic, heartbreaking scene.

What had God promised? "You're going to rule over your brother." That word had guarded Jacob's life from the time he first heard his mother rehearse the story. He must have heard it over and over again as he grew to manhood. But somehow the promises of God hadn't inspired his faith. Or humbled him. Instead, he responded with unbelief and arrogance. Instead of letting God's promise shape His life, he gave in to a convenient deception.

We can all think back on situations where we used manipulation or influence to get what we wanted in our own time or our own way—and we got it. Sometimes our conniving seems to pay off. But Jacob's life reveals God's truth: A blessing can be given and a blessing can be received, but it can never be stolen. You may be thinking, *We just saw it happen! Jacob did get the blessing. He and Rebekah got exactly what they wanted.* Obviously Jacob took something from his brother that Esau could never regain. Isaac said that it had been given. It was done.

But catch the terrible significance of what happened in the stealing. When Jacob finally received the word from Isaac, what should have been a blessing had been toyed with and become twisted. When Jacob finally got the blessing, it had become something else. It had become poisoned by a mother's shame, a father's distrust, and a brother's hatred.

How easily we forget the faithfulness of God. How quickly we think we know what is best and how best to get it!

Think of the deliverance of the children of Israel out of the land of Egypt. Pharaoh's army was buried in the Red Sea, and the Israelites were free on the other side! It was a time of triumph and faith. But the psalmist says, "They soon forgot His works; they did not wait for His counsel, but lusted exceedingly in the wilderness, and tested God in the desert. And He gave them their request" (Psalm 106:13–15, NKJV).

Heard that before? God gave them what they wanted. And God will let you take what He wants to give you too. He'll let you "steal the blessing." But the psalmist goes on to say about the Israelites: "He gave them their request, but sent leanness into their soul."

When the blessing is not received by the patience of faith, then a cancerous condition of the soul eats away at us. It weakens us so that we can't truly experience the blessing. Before long, Jacob was running for his life, leaving all he loved behind. He had a blessing, but he was not a blessed man.

A CHOICE TO TRUST

The Bible is also full of stories of men and women who did wait patiently for the Lord and received the fruitful results of their faith.

One of the most poignant examples is when Abraham bound his only son, Isaac, for sacrifice, as the Lord had commanded. Abraham must have thought, "You promised me a son—and now you're asking me to kill him? Doesn't look like the promise is going to happen...*but I'm going to trust You.*"

Think of Job. "Lord God, You want to kill me? Then kill me...*but I'm still going to trust you.*"

How about the three Hebrew children speaking to Nebuchadnezzar. "You say you're going to put us in the fire if we don't bow down to worship your ninety-foot-tall golden statue. We say, 'We know our God. He can deliver us. He's going to deliver us. But even if He doesn't, we're still not going to bow down to you... *because we're still going to trust Him.*"

In these examples, you can see the heart attitude that can help us to escape deception and keep us free from manipulation. It's a heart and mind that declares: "I will do the right thing. I will not force God's hand. I will wait for His timing alone."

Jacob, of course, eventually returned to Canaan and made peace with his brother but not until he had paid an enormous price. And not until God had so refined his character that he finally became willing to submit to God's way and to God's timing. Only then could God fulfill the original promise that He spoke over the life of this great patriarch of the faith.

Have you operated like Jacob and Rebekah—impatient and fearful that God's promises might be missed if you don't intervene? Have you used spiritual language or Scripture to justify your actions? Maybe your deception is already causing a sense of spiritual cancer eating away at your insides.

Let me assure you that you can experience restoration. It's not too late to respond to His call, to live out your destiny God's way. The step of faith is up to us; but the when and the how of the outcomes are all up to Him.

Admit to God, "I have been deceived and I am deceiving. I am caught in deception, and I want to break free." The One who is called "The Truth" will release you.

Or simply say to God, "I am a manipulator. I am caught in my own unbelief, in a lifestyle of distrust of You. But I want to break free." God can give you the breakthrough. He can heal the leanness of any man or woman's soul. His amazing deliverances can begin right now.

LORD, IN YOUR TIME, IN YOUR WAY

Lord Jesus, You are the One who keeps every promise. May I simply rest in You—and trust in You to fulfill your promises for my life.

I declare with the saints of old, "I know what my God has promised to do, and I have set myself to let Him do it in His time and in His way." Amen.

11

WHEN DREAMS DISAPPEAR

Whatever dream God deposits in your life,
you'll always hit an obstacle so huge
that it will look like your dream can't possibly happen.

The highway loomed before me in the blackness of midnight. I was driving frantically north. A call had come several hours earlier as I finished the business meetings that had taken me to southern California. I left immediately to make the all-night drive back to Oregon.

The thought of losing my wife filled me with terror. Friends had called to say she was behaving irrationally. She seemed to be on a slide toward an emotional breakdown, they said. She needed me *now!*

I didn't care how fast I was driving. I only knew one thing—I had to get home as quickly as humanly possible.

As the lights of Los Angeles faded behind me, pieces of the picture began to come together. Soon I was staring an ugly reality in the face: I was responsible for my wife's confusion and despair. My consuming work schedule and my personal insensitivity had brought her to this point.

Guilt traveled with me like an unwanted passenger as I drove through the night. Somewhere in the darkness of that highway my mind began to rehearse loving moments spent with my wife. What if I never heard her laugh or saw her smile again? No one on earth meant more to me.

A picture of what the future could hold began to develop before my eyes. From what my friends had said on the phone and from my years of pastoral counseling, I knew things were serious. Mental illness could leave me with a wife who wouldn't even recognize me. Suddenly, the dreams I had for our marriage, for our family, for our future seemed to be disappearing into darkness, like the highway in my rearview mirror.

It was one of the bleakest moments of my life.

Each of us in our own way knows how it feels to see something or someone we hold dear slipping away. We've all tasted the fear and helplessness that rise up when we realize that dreams we've cherished and worked for may never come true.

We've already met someone who was terrified that something was slipping away. Remember Jacob? He grappled with God—refusing to let go of Him—because he wanted to get God's best. But here, I'm talking about how we cling to something in our own life—refusing to let go of our own plans, needs, hopes, answers—*because we mistake them for God's best.*

The Bible itself is full of stories of men and women who also came face to face with the probability that their dreams would never be realized. We could name some: Abraham longed for a son, Moses felt called to national leadership, Rachel and Hannah ached for children, and David was compelled to build the Temple.

Joseph was also such a man. In Genesis 37, we read that he was sold into slavery in Egypt by his own brothers. Later we see him betrayed by his Egyptian master's wife and thrown into prison. Yet remarkably, in the face of hopeless circumstances, Joseph held to his belief that God had a special plan for his life.

One thing is certain. People who are following a dream will always face difficulty. An even tougher reality is that resistance is most likely to come from those closest to you—family, friends, your brothers and sisters in Christ. Rarely is it the pagan voice that's lifted up against our dreams. That's why resistance and rejection can be so damaging. When Joseph shared with his family the dreams he received in the night, his brothers scorned him and his father rebuked him.

You may be wondering, "What can I do when my dreams fade? When I face the pit of despair? How should I respond when I'm held captive by circumstances that war against my dreams and threaten to ruin my very life? Where can I find the hope and the courage to go on believing that my God-given dream will come to pass when all that I hold dear is slipping away?"

As I rushed toward my wife's side that night, somewhere between central and northern California God began something in the heart of this troubled pastor that enabled Him to preserve and eventually fulfill my dreams. I found some answers.

> *Resistance is most likely to come from those closest to you.*

God wants us to receive the dream He has for our lives. But just as importantly, we need to understand how to withstand the onslaught that will attempt to destroy that dream. It's one thing to have a God-given dream deposited in your heart; it's quite another thing to embrace the dream and to keep it.

THE TIME TO GIVE UP

When you find yourself caught in the enemy's web of deception or thrown into your own personal pit of rejection, I recommend that you give up! Does that response surprise you? It's so simple that people often miss it! Giving up is usually the last thing we do.

When you find yourself in a hole—stop digging! Get rid of all shovels. Of course, often you want out so desperately that the natural urge is to keep digging. Something rises up, and you hear yourself shouting to the sky, "I'll never give up! I'll never let go of my dream!"

Sounds brave, but it's actually very stupid. The more strength you call upon, the more determination you show while you are in the pit, the deeper you dig yourself into the hole. You feel better because you're working so furiously, but the pit only gets deeper.

Let's look at the big picture again: God has dreams for your life. Dreams that are forever settled in heaven. Dreams that have been in His heart since He first imagined you. Dreams intended to give you meaning and purpose, a destiny, a calling, a personal assignment.

But whatever dream God deposits into your life, whatever eternal plan He invites you to be a part of, you'll always hit an obstacle so huge that it will look like the dream can't possibly happen. You won't see any way around the obstacle, over it, or through it. Your pit is just too deep. And in the midst of those painful, stressful, humiliating circumstances, God will ask you to give up.

You lose when you fight your circumstances, determined to win. You win when you give up to God.

Of course, you should expect confusion, because your surrender to God can feel like a surrender of your dream. But it isn't. If you know the dream is really from God, then you can offer it back to Him. Just cry out to God, "I'm in a pit, and I can't make this thing happen. Only You can. Here are my dreams. I surrender."

Don't give up to the enemy or to the circumstances. Give up to your Father, the One who is greater than any circumstance. Say, "You are my God. You are greater than any of these circumstances. I place them all in Your loving hands. I place my life and this dream in Your hands."

We only receive the grace that empowers us to resist the enemy when we humble ourselves and submit to God. The only way to discover the incredible potential of the power that makes the dream possible is through surrender.

HOLD ON TO HOPE

When Joseph hit his obstacles, how easy it would have been for him to give in to bitterness, to say, "Look at me—I deserve better than this." After all, he knew he was the favored son. He knew he had a destiny from God. Something or someone had gone wrong—and as far as he could tell, it wasn't him. There he was in a dark prison cell, betrayed by those who were supposed to love him. Yet instead of anger or whining, we see a young man who accepts what is dealt him and does what he can before God. Genesis 40 shows Joseph humbly using his gifts to serve others in prison—without notice or reward.

We're good at running our experience through our Life Analyzer—and coming up with very misleading data. For example, we can look at failures or loss and decide that our chances for destiny are lost too. Or we can conclude that we never were who we thought we were in God's kingdom. Or maybe we decide that now we deserve that easy-to-reach and terribly addictive narcotic called self-pity.

> *We're good at running our experiences through our Life Analyzer—and coming up with very misleading data.*

When you find yourself in a pit, remember you still have a future. That is the reality that matters most. When Jerusalem was enduring a terrible siege by the armies of Babylon, God wanted them to remember His dream for them: "I know the plans I have for you,… plans to prosper you and not to harm you, plans to give you hope and a future" (Jeremiah 29:11, NIV).

When all the dust settles and all your dreams have been blown away, God's Word remains true. You have a future because you are a child of God.

If your husband is gone and your dreams for the kind of home you thought you ought to have, or wanted to have, are gone with him—you still have a future.

If your wife has left and in that terrible rejection your psyche has been bruised and mutilated, I tell you in Jesus—you still have a future.

If your business is failing, I say to you—you have a future.

Say to God, the Maker and Giver of dreams, "If my dream wasn't of You, then I don't want it because I belong to You. If my dream wasn't of You, then I know You will make something good come out of this pit. Something better for me. I believe my future is in You."

This is the truth I discovered as I made the long trek home that dark February night.

RELEASING HIS POWER

As I drove, it became very dark in the car. Not the darkness of night, but a darkness that I knew was the presence of evil. I wanted so much to hold on to my dreams, to never let go. But something began to well up from inside me, something even stronger than my frantic desire to hold on.

And soon I heard myself saying: "Lord, if this circumstance in my life and in Kay's life is real, and if it is going to be this way the rest of our lives, then I give up to You. If I have to spend the rest of my days caring for a wife who does not recognize me, who cannot relate to me, who cannot communicate with me, then I'll do it. I love her. I love you. I belong to You. I give up."

From that moment, the darkness was gone. You win when you give up to God.

As it turned out, God was using a health challenge in my wife's life to get my attention. But my attention was the real problem—not my wife's health; she recovered well from her season of stress. That night, I had many miles to contemplate what the Lord was trying to show me. And in the weeks ahead, I followed through with some painful but very necessary decisions about priorities in our home.

And what have I learned that I could pass on to you?

Stop arguing with your circumstances.

Stop telling God where you don't belong and what you don't deserve.

Stop doing battle with God's sovereign purposes in your life.

Instead, embrace the gift of surrender, the gift of submission. It's a gift the Holy Spirit will give you if you'll give up to God. He can release His power in your life if you'll start making choices with your promised future in mind. And if you'll act out of what you know is the favor of God resting on you—because of who you are in Jesus Christ—then you will be allowing the One who gave you that original, treasured dream to make it come to pass for you.

LORD OF DARK HIGHWAYS

Lord Jesus, I give up to You.

I let go to You all my strivings, my expectations, my bitterness, my stubbornness. I want Your promised future for my life.

I belong to You.

Let Your praises be the strength of my life. Amen.

12
SONGS AT MIDNIGHT

When you begin to make those first sounds of trust, it is beautiful
music. You are surrounding others with songs of deliverance.

You might think of it as Scripture's most famous
jailbreak story. You're probably familiar with the
account in Acts of Paul and Silas's night in the Philippian prison (Acts 16:16–40). The sights and sounds of
that story seem to stay with us, maybe even haunt us.

Picture this: Afternoon. The marketplace at Philippi
under a blistering Macedonian sun. Angry crowds
cheer on the floggers as the whips cut—again and
again—into the bare backs of Paul and Silas. The
groans of the two preachers as they writhe naked,
bleeding, and alone in the dust. The crowd backs off
to let the jailers drag the men away. A boy darts forward to spit in their bloodied faces.

A moment of severe persecution. It stays in the
mind.

Or picture this: A few minutes after midnight.
Suddenly an earthquake hits the Philippian jail with a
series of terrible jolts. Rocks fall, dust flies. As man-
acled prisoners scream for help in the darkness, they
notice a strange sight. All the prison doors are swing-
ing open on their hinges. Everyone's chains have fallen

off; everyone—including Paul and Silas—is free to go. The terrified jailer has decided to die by falling on his own sword, apparently unaware of the strangest sight of all—no one is leaving.

Or this: A few minutes later, the jailer is on his knees before Paul and Silas crying out, "Sirs! What must I do to be saved?" As the night rolls on toward morning, the picture changes: The jailer is washing and bandaging the two men's wounds. And by morning light, he and his whole household are being baptized into the family of God—in jail!

I encourage you to read the entire account in Acts 16, but in this context I want to look carefully at just one verse. It describes the sights and sounds of the most memorable and exciting scene of this whole story: "And at midnight Paul and Silas prayed, and sang praises unto God, and the prisoners heard them" (Acts 16:25, KJV).

In this turning-point verse, I want you to see what God might say to you about why we praise and how we praise. You see, there is a kind of praise that causes earthquakes. This praise is birthed deep in our souls by God to honor Him, to bless us, and to serve as a spiritual call to others around us.

How does this kind of praise happen?

When the jailer asks "What must I do to be saved?" we realize instantly that he knew something important about Paul and Silas. He knew that he wasn't dealing with a normal event—even a normal, disastrous earthquake. He had made an immediate connection between the events in his prison and the truth of Paul and Silas's message.

WORSHIP IN TROUBLED TIMES

Earthquake praise rises from our lips when we are in the midst of trouble. And that's the thing that catches everybody's imagination in this story—praise in the dark, praise from broken, bleeding lips and chipped teeth, praise from the dungeon of a strange city, praise...and then the first tremendous wrenching of the earth!

But consider this: These two heroes of the New Testament had been in prison for hours since their public punishment took place—hours when, apparently, no praises left their mouth. Hours when praise just wasn't going to happen, even from an apostle.

That comforts me.

If you're like me, you feel slightly guilty when something bad happens and your first response is *anything but* praise. At those times, we suffer from a damaging idea about God. We're reeling from a crisis of some sort, but we picture God up in heaven saying, "OK, good to see Roy is finally starting to praise, but it took him awhile to get his act together. Think I'll just let him stew in his juices for a while."

But that's not the attitude of heaven. God is not removed from our pain. When the whips are slicing across Silas's back, the Father is wincing. When Paul takes another, the Father flinches—in the same way that Jesus wept at Lazarus's tomb.

Now they're in the dark prison. It's cold and you can hear the rats squeaking, the water dripping; you can smell the stench. But is God up in heaven waiting for a spiritually "correct" response? No. The Holy Spirit is with them. He is right there, offering comfort.

Singing at midnight is true worship from real people in trouble, who feel it in every nerve and sinew—not spiritual idealists who don't really experience trouble. We're always limited by our bodies and emotions. Do we really think this fact is a surprise to God? He knows you and me—and is deeply committed to us—as human beings, His physical creations. We can be comforted to know that earthquake praise may be delayed praise.

We've spent some time with Joseph's story. It's easy to remember his ringing declaration, "You intended to harm me, but God intended it for good." But don't forget or overlook the fact that he made that statement *decades* after the offense.

God is so very patient with us. Some of you have been in situations for more than just hours and you haven't praised yet. Perhaps it's been weeks, months, or years. Perhaps your "public beating" came when you were a grade-schooler and you're a mature woman now. Perhaps it came when you were a strapping young man with a promising career ahead—and now you're feeling the aches and limitations of later life.

God has not given up on you even though you have yet to lift your voice in praise about the painful drubbing that has happened to you. God has not abandoned you. He's not docking you for not being someone else. But He is patiently calling you to something greater. He's waiting to turn your world upside down—if you're willing.

> *God has not given up on you even though you have yet to lift your voice in praise about the painful drubbing that has happened to you.*

WHEN PRISONERS LISTEN

At midnight in Philippi, a sound began. Not music, really. Probably something between a croak and a groan. But soon it was recognizable as praise. Many think these two Jewish Christians would have sung a psalm. Suppose they sang Psalm 46: "God is our refuge and strength, an ever present help in trouble. Therefore we will not fear, though the earth give way" (46:1, NIV).

What started as a croak soon took on the lilting music of worship. As they sang, their thoughts gradually turned away from the stench of the prison to memories of the fragrance of temple incense, from the sound of clanking chains to the singing of young believers in Antioch, from the agony of untreated wounds to the joy of their soon returning Lord.

And the prisoners listened.

For me it's sobering to realize how closely the people with whom we work or go to school watch and listen to our lives. We'd like to get away from this kind of scrutiny sometimes, but we can't. People are checking us out all the time.

Do you come off like a goody two-shoes, saying religious things like "Praise the Lord" and "Hallelujah" all the time? That antiseptic example is probably not going to affect nonbelievers. Doing the religious thing for someone else's benefit doesn't help anyone.

What makes prisoners listen? To me, the compelling quality of Paul and Silas's praise was that the men were in the same cells, experiencing the same life as the other prisoners. In fact, maybe the other prisoners thought their situations weren't so bad after all compared to the shape Paul and Silas were in.

When you share a life trauma with nonbelievers, when they can see you begin to move through it, showing however imperfectly your faith and confidence in a good God—they *will* listen.

WHEN GOD BECOMES REAL

Don't you wonder why, if all the doors were open and all the chains were gone, the prisoners didn't make a break for freedom?

Some scholars think God put angels at the doors. But I think the prisoners were like the jailer—they knew this wasn't just an earthquake. The coincidences were too powerful to ignore: Two men who were preaching about a strange God had been beaten to a pulp and thrown in jail. Then, as these two strangers sang praises, an earthquake had broken open the jail. Two and two made four.

When we praise in the middle of calamity, we have an incredible impact on others, especially prisoners of all types. Why? We demonstrate for them the kind of life that they have always longed for and don't have—*that they were willing to commit crimes to get.*

One day when I pulled in at my usual store to buy gas, the attendant took my credit card, then looked at me and said, "You're the guy on TV, aren't ya? I watch you every now and then."

"All right," I said. "Great to hear it."

He seemed to want to talk. He volunteered that he didn't go to church anymore, but went on to say that he was having problems with lust. "I'm married and I've never slept with another woman besides my wife," he said. "But I have a lot of this stuff going on in my head."

"You know, I fight with stuff like that too," I said.

His mouth dropped open. I guess his preconceptions about preachers as human beings had just taken a big hit. Maybe he had thought preachers have children by immaculate conception.

While he sorted out his reactions, I plunged straight ahead. "The only thing I've found is to come to Jesus as a man, to give yourself over to Him completely, and to invite Him to begin to help you deal with those kinds of images," I said. "Because it got started someplace. He is the only one who can help you clean up your mind."

As I shared my faith with him, I could tell his view about Christians was getting a thorough working over. I went from "one of those guys on TV who talk about God" to a customer who seemed to understand and care about his life. By then, other customers were lining up behind me, but the attendant just wanted to talk.

You see, prisoners listen. But not to wardens. Prisoners listen to prisoners—prisoners who aren't phonies about the bad things that happen in life, who may not be able to praise for some time after a trauma. Who may not be able to make all the "correct" praise sounds—whatever those are.

When you begin to make those first sounds of trust, it is beautiful music—no matter what your voice is like! The Bible says you are surrounding others with songs of deliverance. You are making the sounds of freedom, even though you may still be in pain or bondage or dealing with many difficulties.

Prisoners are listening—and they won't leave.

When you begin to make those first sounds of trust, it is beautiful music—no matter what your voice is like! You are surrounding others with songs of deliverance.

PRAISE FOR FREE

When I was a teenager attending a youth rally, I heard somebody preach on this story of Paul and Silas in jail. There were about 250–300 of us at the event. The preacher wanted us to "exercise our praise muscles," he said. He wanted us to see the connection between our praise and God's actions. At the end of the service, he called us down to the front to give "earthquake praise."

We almost tore the place apart—it was fun, and it was loud, and everybody cried with joy.

But no earthquakes happened.

Why?

I think if you read the story carefully, you'll catch what I caught only years later. If you praise in order to cause an earthquake, best bets are you'll never see one.

I don't think for a moment that Silas said to Paul:

"Let's go to plan number 32-a—'Earthquake.'"

On the contrary, I believe they expected to rot in that Macedonian jail for a very long time, and possibly die there. I think one said to the other, "Well, it looks like this is it." Maybe Silas tried to coax a laugh out of Paul with a little teasing: "You and your visions—we followed God and look where it got us."

Then one of them just started. From deep in a soul untouched by whips or jeers or blows or spitting or circumstances of any kind came forth a sound. And it was the sound of praises to the Lord Jesus.

Maybe it was just moaning at first. But soon the men were singing words of worship:

> I lift my voice to You, my God, and sing songs of praise even though I'm in jail.
>
> I lift my voice of praise to You even though I've just been beaten and it sure sounds like they're going to kill us tomorrow.
>
> I praise You, I praise You, Jesus, because You're worthy to be praised, not to get You to do something. I praise You. I worship You.
>
> I sing songs of deliverance. Hallelujah, Lord!

Nothing in their praise was designed to manipulate God. And that, I think, is the kind of praise that causes earthquakes.

Remember the three Hebrew men in Babylon: "We know our God is able to deliver us," they said to King Nebuchadnezzar. "But even if He doesn't, we're not bowing down." Their declaration wasn't intended to maneuver God into a corner, or squeeze anything out of Him. How often we make statements of faith to get something from God when we could be believing that He is acting—and that our praise is the best possible way to cooperate with His faithfulness and power.

Can you imagine this: the countenance of Jesus when one of the men started to sing? "Let's praise," one of them says. "I hurt so bad I can't even move, but let's praise." Can you imagine the joy of God in the pure thankfulness of these disciples?

Your pure praise response makes a difference not in just your own life but in the spiritual dimension. In her book *Affliction,* Edith Schaeffer described the spiritual battlefield that each of us participates in daily. When we're in moments of pain and terror, when our hearts are downcast, when things don't go the way we planned—at those moments we have access to great power. For when we will finally pull ourselves up and say, "I praise You anyway, Lord!" and go on—at that moment the tide of the battle shifts in favor of the heavenly forces.

Pure worship is the very kind of praise that causes the Father to say, "Watch this!"

CALLED TO A FUTURE

I can assure this—if you make decisions to follow God, to live as He originally intended, sooner or later you are going to wind up in jail. But the faithfulness of God will work with you, and about midnight somewhere along the line it will dawn on you—in any situation, in any darkness or pain, you can praise.

Singing at midnight is not about the circumstances that bring us down. It is about the God who lifts us up with love and hope. We don't praise to change the situation. We praise because He deserves our sincere praise *whatever* the situation.

You might be in your midnight hour right now, stretched out on the stones of rejection or pain or disappointment. As you meditate on the biblical characters and spiritual truths we've encountered, listen for a word from the Lord as you wait on these stones. Let God's presence minister to you—there's no rush to make up some response. These stones have stories:

Paul and Silas bled here in their chains, and sang songs of freedom too.

> *We don't praise to change the situation.*
> *We praise because He deserves our sincere praise*
> *whatever the situation.*

Joseph, the dreamer of God's dreams, was here in

jail before you. He spent years humbly doing good in stone cells like these. And Jacob, along with Isaac and Rebekah, struggled with God on stones like these because nothing less than God's best was good enough.

Peter and John, the fishermen with Galilee's best fishing stories, were here before you bringing the gospel to the imprisoned, broken, and forgotten ones of the world.

Are you ready to begin to praise, even if you spend the rest of your life in a physical, emotional, or financial jail of some kind? Start with a raspy groan, a silly croak—solely because of who God is, how good He's been to you all these years, how mighty are His works.

Praise—sincere, human, and without strings attached—is the sound you make when you are wholeheartedly answering God's call to your soul. And the sound of your praise is always a powerful means that God uses to speak words of life to those around you.

Once you answer God's invitation, there is no telling what He will do.

IT IS GOOD TO PRAISE THE LORD

It is good to praise the Lord, and make music to Your name, O Most High;

It is good to praise the Lord.

Proclaim Your love in the morning and Your faithfulness at night.

It is good, it is good to praise the Lord. Amen.

PRAISE THE NAME OF JESUS

Praise the name of Jesus!
Praise the name of Jesus!
He's my rock
He's my fortress,
He's my deliverer,
in Him will I trust.
Praise the name of Jesus!

ROY HICKS JR.

To obtain an audiocassette of original sermons found in *A Small Book about God,* please indicate chapter title and send $5.00 per sermon to:

Faith Center
Attn: Resource Center
1410 West 13th
Eugene, Oregon 97402
or
Call (541)686-9244
Fax (541)465-9121